Advance Praise for: A World of Hurt
by Mary Reynolds Powell

"Mary personifies the tender mercy of all nurses thrust into combat. Her book needs to be read by young America today, for it was yesterday's young America that gave the best they had in a troubled land in a troubled time."

– **James Banks**, Ph.D., Ohio Professor of the Year 1994, 1997 Professor Emeritus of History, Cuyahoga Community College

. . . .

"This work is a gripping human story which reminds me of *Paco's Story; Dispatches; A Rumor of War* and *Home Before Morning*, all great contributions about the insanity of the Vietnam War...Powell's book is a passionate, moving and among the 'must' read of human tragedy, sorrow, and humor which are embedded in chaos and existential malaise of the 'heart of darkness' known some 35 years later as, the Vietnam War."

– **John P. Wilson**, Ph.D., Professor of Psychology, Cleveland State University and President, Forensic Center for Traumatic Stress, Cleveland Heights, OH

. . . .

"A work of rare insight and lasting importance... perhaps the most sensitive and eloquent book ever to examine nursing in Vietnam."

– **Robert K. Brigham**, Associate Professor of History, Vassar College and author of *Argument Without End: In Search of Answers to the Vietnam War*

...more praise...

"Anyone who questions the extreme stress placed on the military nurses who served in the Vietnam War should read *A World of Hurt: Between Innocence and Arrogance in Vietnam*. The heartbreaking duty Mary Reynolds and every other nurse at the 24th Evacuation Hospital in Long Binh faced is told with a vividness that illustrates the moral dilemmas and profound losses found in Vietnam, in any war."

– **Elizabeth M. Norman**, PhD., NYU, author of *We Band of Angles: The Untold Story of American Nurses Trapped on Bataan by the Japanese.*

• • • •

"Mary Reynolds Powell has been telling her story for many years in forums ranging from high school assemblies and churches to lunch meetings of the Junior League. Now, she shares with thousands of readers her journey of memory and inquiry into the meaning of the American experience in Vietnam... Twenty-five years after the final withdrawal of American forces from Vietnam, her powerful memoir serves to remind all of us of the perils of repressed memories and unacknowledged responsibility. My students never fail to be deeply moved by Mary's passion and sincerity."

– **Claudia Boatright**, Department of History, Laurel School, Shaker Heights, OH

• • • •

...still more praise...

"The service of American women – civilian and military – in Vietnam has too long lived in the shadows of our national consciousness. Mary Reynolds Powell's powerfully written account of her service in Vietnam and its effect on her life helps to bring that service into the clear place of understanding and honor that it deserves."

– **Clarence R. Wyatt**, Professor of History, Pottinger Distinguished Associate, Centre College and author of *Paper Soldiers: The American Press and the Vietnam War*

• • • •

"Mary Reynolds Powell has written a work of such quiet devastation it reflects the Vietnam War itself. She does not merely tell you of the horror of war, she takes you by the hand and leads you into it, step by measured step, until "the kids" of her wards become your own. The tiniest act of mercy, a cup of orange juice, fills your heart until it breaks along with hers and those of her comrades at the 24th Evacuation Hospital. You have to put the book down again and again to build the strength necessary to read it. This is not merely a work of non-fiction, it is a prayer – a plea to anyone who will listen, there is nothing acceptable in the arrogance of throwing the children of one country against the children of another in the blood of the foolish inability of leaders to resolve their differences. Don't talk of putting this incredible piece of literature in the hands of the leaders of our country before they vote one more dollar for military destruction – just do it!"

– **Lynda Van Devanter**, author of *Home Before Morning: The Story of an Army Nurse in Vietnam* and co-editor of *Visions of War, Dreams of Peace: Writings of Women in the Vietnam War.*

• • • •

A WORLD OF HURT

Mary Reynolds Powell

April 25, 2000 First Edition

ISBN: 0-9665319-5-7

Library of Congress Catalog Card Number: 00-100344

Cover Design by Denny Wendell
Upper Back Cover Photo by Douglas Powell
Lower Back Cover Photo by Herbert Ascherman
Layout by Francine Smith

Greenleaf Enterprises
P.O. Box 291
Chesterland, Ohio 44026

Printed in the U.S.A.

Published in the United States by
Greenleaf Enterprises, Cleveland, Ohio.

www.greenleafenterprises.com

DEDICATION
· · · · · · · ·

for Doug
who has always understood

for Jessica, Cathy and Steven
that they may understand

and for the guys in the blue pajamas

IN MEMORIAM
· · · · · · · ·

Frank H. Chamberlin, Col, MC, USA
1929-1992

A percentage of the proceeds from the sale of this book will be donated by the author to the Vietnam Women's Memorial Project, Inc. The VWMP is not responsible for the contents of this book and has no role in its creation. For further information about this organization, readers can contact:

Vietnam Women's Memorial Project, Inc.
2001 "S" Street NW
Suite #610
Washington, DC   20009

> This book is the product of memories;
> we wish we remembered more.
> Some of the names in this book have been changed.

Table of Contents

FOREWORD

• • • • • • • •

COL DAVID H. HACKWORTH, US ARMY (RET.)

Since the last American helicopter lifted off the roof of the U.S. Embassy in Saigon, twenty-five years have passed. Thousands of books have now been written about the Vietnam War, most by historians or the men that did the fighting, or the generals and their apologists trying to put a winning face on what went down in that bad war.

I suspect the historians have tried to bring clarity, understanding and a certain tidiness to a conflict that ripped America apart and that will probably not go away until those who lived through that decade of fire have gone to their maker.

And if my experience in writing *About Face* is a guide, most of the grunts (infantry soldiers) wrote their stories to try to scrub the war from their souls or tell it like it was down where the killing took place.

But the generals and their men — rationalizers and revisionists for the Vietnam War such as the late Colonel Harry Summers — have tried to spin the disastrous defeat into victory. They say there really was "light at the end of the tunnel" and that we did in fact win the war. In reality, it was a war that was as unwinnable, at least the way their bosses fought it, as it was morally wrong.

Their standard line is preached by arch-conservative Fred Barnes, who believes that America was right to intervene militarily (in Vietnam), concluding that the worldwide consequences would have been far worse for the non-Communist world if it hadn't. He says General William Westmoreland's strategy of using massive force to 'search and destroy' and to maximize the enemy's death toll was bound to fail. But he insists that the war was winnable because of the strategy of Westmoreland's successor, General Creighton Abrams. He even asserts it had actually been won by sometime in 1970, when, he alleges, the Viet Cong and North Vietnamese had all but been snuffed out as major threats in South Vietnam. He insists that the war was ultimately lost not because of limits on the American military but because American support for South Vietnam was removed.

I was in Vietnam from 1965 to 1971, in the field down where the dying occurs. The conditions and situation Barnes describes simply never existed. On the contrary, each year we got weaker while our supposedly "snuffed out" opponent grew stronger.

Sadly, the revisionists are gaining momentum, and those who continue to shout "wrong, wrong, wrong" are being painted as wild-eyed, card-carrying liberals rather than the truth-tellers they in fact are. Even many vets who fought there and know better are buying into the standard revisionist line that "We won all the battles, but lost the war." Perhaps they're allowing themselves to be duped because they're either into denial or want to be perceived as winners the way their dads were after WW II.

Meanwhile, today's youth haven't a clue about the Vietnam War. A Vietnam veterans' organization recently reported that one third of American students age 12 to 17 haven't received any instruction on the war and can't find Vietnam on a map. Over seventy-five percent of them think that the U.S. won a decisive victory even though they have relatives who fought in the war.

Mary Reynolds Powell's powerful book is the perfect anti dote to blow the revisionists out of the water — with the facts, eloquently presented. Not only is it beautifully written, it's a riveting and very moving insider's view of what goes on in field hospitals in combat zones. From inside the wards, the operating rooms, the triage points, the reader will experience the horror, the futility, the waste of war and for sure won't find it $M*A*S*H$ funny. You'll see dedicated medics — doctors, nurses, corpsmen — fighting to save lives along with all the other wonderful folks who too often become scarred for life while repairing the damage done by man's need to resolve conflict with the military solution.

Frequently, while reading former Army nurse Powell's gut-wrenching story, which is composed of one potent anecdote after another, I found tears running down my face. "The soldier in the ICU was no more than a boy and he was dying," she writes. "He had multiple abdominal wounds. Tubes connected him to equipment around him. One morning at about five, he asked [nurse] Stephanie [Genthon] for a glass of orange juice. 'I told him he couldn't have anything to drink,' she tearfully explained. He answered, 'Stephanie, I'm dead anyway. It doesn't matter.' 'OK' she said. 'Let me see.' She called the doctor, who said 'No,' so Stephanie gave him nothing. Fifteen minutes later he was dead."

When soldiers on the Vietnam battlefield witnessed a platoon brother get chopped down, they generally only saw a dark patch on a uniform and heard the cry of "medic!" The platoon "doc" did what he does, medevac rolled in and suddenly their friend was gone. They seldom shared the long-term horror, listened to the days and nights of screaming or got to watch as the bodybags were moved to the morgue.

It's always the hospital medics who see it all as it's happening. And then I suspect this nightmare plays on and on for the rest of their lives.

Mary's book should be required reading by all lawmakers just prior to their signing off on a declaration of war. When they're confronted with the hard and cruel consequences of their actions, maybe they won't be so eager to try and resolve conflict with more of the same.

Maybe they'll work harder to find a peaceful solution. Maybe they'll not buy into the revisionists' line that we won the war. Maybe they'll give George Santayana's too often ignored comment, "Those who cannot remember the past are condemned to repeat it" more respect than was the case in Somalia in 1993 when 44 Americans were killed and almost 500 wounded because our Army's learned nothing from the tragedy of Vietnam.

David Hackworth

Author: *About Face, Hazardous Duty,* and *The Price of Honor*

PROLOGUE

• • • • • • • •

The talk had already started when I arrived, so I quickly slipped into a rear aisle seat. It was May, 1990, and I was there to hear the final presentation of a three-day Vietnam Retrospective sponsored by the State University of New York at Binghamton. At the front of the room, the speaker, a retired colonel, was discussing "The Vietnam War from a Military Perspective." Twenty years before, I had been a U.S. Army nurse in Vietnam. Because I left the Army within ten hours of my return to the States, I had never heard someone in the military analyze the war that had so affected my life. I was eager to hear what he had to say.

In the years before my arrival in Vietnam, my opinion of the war had undergone a transformation paralleling that of many Americans. In October, 1965, my brother, a Naval Academy graduate, was in Vietnam, and I marched in a New York City parade backing the war. I was proud of my father, who served on our local draft board. Exactly four years later, in October of 1969, I wore a black armband in support of the national peace moratorium and criticized my father for what he did. Sad to say, my opposition to the war was not ideological. It was due, rather, to the loss of American lives. Nightly TV footage of caskets occupied by people my age had taken its toll on me. Half the names on our church honor roll belonged to boys who had sat in the back rows of my elementary school class in the Bronx. Even when I was sent to Vietnam in November, 1970, I understood little of the war. I just hoped it would end.

By the time I left Southeast Asia a year later, I was convinced that everything about U.S. involvement was wrong. During my tour, I witnessed the final stages of an arrogant effort fueled for years by American ignorance of Vietnamese culture and official deception of the American public. In March, 1971, U.S. soldiers went on trial for war crimes at My Lai. In June, the *Pentagon Papers* documented the lie on which the war had been built. Excerpts of the book in the *New York Times* made my copy a hot commodity on the hospital ward. Nurses, doctors, corpsmen and even the patients asked to read it. In October, a single candidate ran in the Vietnamese presidential election: Nguyen Van Thieu, a man who brutally smashed his opposition and allegedly funded his campaign with drug money. The democracy for which tens of thousands of Americans had died was manifestly a sham. I watched the worst America had to offer destroy the people we had come to "save." I saw the proliferation of black-marketeering, prostitution and drug abuse. I witnessed military pride give way to moral disintegration. And worst of all, I, and everyone else stationed in Vietnam, knew American kids were being wasted in a war that had no meaning.

That day in Binghamton, I expected the colonel to discuss what military leaders had learned from their experience. I thought he would say something on the order of, "We thought 'x', so we did 'y', but our assumptions were wrong, so 'z' happened." Instead, he gave a textbook presentation that focused on military tactics in the abstract, much like a football coach analyzing a playbook. Political and cultural realities that were central to the war meant little to him. The only reason he even acknowledged them was to blame them for getting in the way of military science.

Most upsetting to me, he refused to accept responsibility for the role played by the military command in Vietnam. He intimated everyone but the military was guilty for what had happened: civilian authorities, the American people, the Viet Cong, the North Vietnamese Army, the Vietnamese people, their geography, and even the stars. The American generals, he said, were forced to fight without a mission, a strategy, or the support of the country. Consequently, they lost the war, though they never lost a battle. He implied that they were caught in an accident of history, unable to influence circumstances. He said simply, "We were the wrong people in the wrong place at the wrong time."

The colonel did not explain how senior officers with no mission, strategy, or support engineered a ten-year effort that sent three million Americans to war and almost sixty-thousand to their deaths. He did not mention that poor military leadership led to troop demoralization, or that military policies compromised the safety of troops in the field. He ignored military corruption, as well as military exploitation and abuse of the Vietnamese people. In short, the colonel chose to forget the war I saw in 1971.

Questions followed his talk. A slender man with graying hair sat quietly with his arm raised, waiting to be recognized. When called upon, he identified himself as a Vietnam veteran who, during his tour of duty and for twenty years after, believed he had done the right thing in Vietnam. Recently, however, he had begun to question the actions of the U.S., and he felt unsure about his role in the war. He said he was confused by the speaker's assertion that military leaders had been powerless. In response, the colonel gave the veteran a benign smile, broadened it to include the audience, and then steered his answer right past the question and into platitudes about service to country. The vet's shoulders slumped.

The veteran revealed such vulnerability that I wanted to put my arms around him to shield him from the speaker's arrogance. As the colonel finished his final comments, I made my way through the crowd to the veteran's side. I knelt next to him, placed my hand on his shoulder, turned to face him, and broke down. Words would not come. Sobs engulfed me. His arm circled my shoulder. With my pain came the startling realization that I had been in this position before. Twenty years earlier, I had wanted to protect the innocent kids in blue pajamas from the arrogant system that sent them to war. Then, I had to stifle my emotions to survive. This time I could feel the pain. This time I could cry.

• • • •

What follows is an account of my own experience in Vietnam as well as the stories of seven friends who served with me. Though we came from diverse backgrounds and held different positions in the military, we shared the Vietnam War of 1971.

• • • •

CHAPTER ONE

•   •   •   •   •   •   •

"Oh-h-h shit… what have I gotten myself into?"

"Don't worry," said the attractive red-headed recruiter, "By the time you're ready for the Army, we won't be in Vietnam." I was in her New York City office investigating a tuition assistance plan for student nurses—one year of assistance meant a two-year commitment to the military after college. She suggested that I might be sent to hospitals in San Francisco, Hawaii or even London. Her reassurance was not meant to deceive me. It was late 1967, and most Americans, even those in government, would have agreed that we would be out of Vietnam soon. Four months later, the Tet offensive of January,1968, shattered the illusion of an early exit from the war. But at the same time, it sparked widespread opposition to the conflict by mainstream America. In March, when President Lyndon Johnson announced he would not run for re-election in order to devote his energy to ending the war, I was convinced I would never see Southeast Asia. I joined the program in May, 1968, received financial assistance for my senior year, and began basic training twenty months later, after I had passed New York State Nursing Boards.

Valley Forge General Hospital in Pennsylvania was my first assignment. The hospital, built during World War II, was re-activated for the Korean War and again for Vietnam. The general surgery, orthopedic, urological and plastic surgery wards were filled with battle casualties. Recuperating soldiers whose legs had been amputated held daily wheelchair races up and down its wide central corridor and mess hall ramps. Despite these reminders, the war stayed at the periphery of my life because I worked in the pediatric unit. The kids— children of military personnel in the region— were great, and I would have been happy to stay with them for my full tour. But after eight months, a computer in an Army personnel office found me. Now, I was one of ten women officers boarding a midnight flight at California's Travis Air Force Base. My luggage was tagged for war, and my stomach had turned to lead.

The bright lights of the terminal bathed the United Airlines jet as we climbed its stairs to meet smiling stewardesses. They might just as easily have been sending us on a vacation. Like the men who earlier had checked our bags, they acted as though we were on a routine flight. I sought my seat— a middle one between two immense soldiers— reassuring myself, "OK... so far... so good..." I could not think beyond the moment. Others seemed to feel the same way. Conversation, as the more than two-hundred-fifty of us took our seats, was subdued and hesitant. Nervous laughter erupted intermittently. When the plane took off, relief filled the cabin, and people started talking to each other. Whatever our fate, at least the "good-byes" were behind us. A flight attendant passed out small milk cartons with the first meal. Across the aisle from me, a soldier grabbed three cartons in each hand. He advised me to do the same. "You won't see real milk for a year," he said with a wide grin.

Our plane flew before the sun across the Pacific. At our first stop, Hawaii, we watched the sun rise over Diamond Head. At midday, we touched down on an island that was little more than a runway surrounded by blue Pacific Ocean. My ankles had begun to swell. My feet, squeezed into high-heeled pumps, throbbed. Despite the destination, I was increasingly anxious for the trip to be over. Then, in Okinawa, we collided with our future.

It was the final stop before Vietnam. Because of airport construction, our path to the terminal wound through a constricted walkway, made even narrower by a single file of Marines walking past us to their "freedom bird," the plane that would take them home to the States. Idle chatter stopped. Silence fell over us. We exchanged no friendly greetings or nods with the Marines. As they filed by, we found ourselves staring into the oldest eyes we had ever seen. These were young men— younger than I— but their eyes were ancient, their faces blank.

We passed the rest of the flight in silence. As each mile brought us closer to the war, we withdrew into private thoughts. Flight attendants served our last meal while we watched the film *Good-bye Mr. Chips*. At two in the afternoon, twenty-five hours after taking off from Travis, word circulated that we had entered Vietnam airspace. Soldiers raised the small shades on the airline windows. Sunlight streamed into the cabin, dulling the on-screen images of Peter O'Toole and Petula Clark. It did not matter, because no one was watching the screen. Soldiers seated at windows pressed against them while their row companions leaned over their shoulders to catch a glimpse of what lay below. Like the others, I gazed in silence. "Oh-h-h shit," I thought, "What have I gotten myself into?"

The plane landed at the Bien Hoa Air Force Base, eighteen miles northeast of Saigon. Adjacent to the airbase were the Bien Hoa Army Base and Long Binh Post, at forty-six square miles the largest enclosed Army base in the world. Together, the three facilities equaled a good-sized U.S. city. During our descent, we saw mile upon mile of defoliated earth, dusty roads, wooden buildings, quonset huts, trailer homes, overhead electrical wires and TV antennas. Water buffalo grazed on the meager grass that surrounded each military base. Shacks, home to some of the 30,000 Vietnamese workers who entered the bases daily, stood outside the perimeter of the American "metropolis." A smoggy haze hung close to the earth.

The plane taxied to a stop. Two soldiers in jungle fatigues and dark berets entered the cabin. Carrying sidearms and M-16 rifles, they walked the full length of the center aisle, returned to the front and instructed us to leave. Should we be fired on as we crossed the tarmac, we were to run into the dubious security of the open air terminal and throw ourselves onto the floor. With their melodramatic style, the soldiers opened our eyes to the active war being waged in November, 1970. We exited the plane with the individual determination of sheep. Years later, I learned that the runway at Bien Hoa was rocketed the day after I arrived.

· · · ·

CHAPTER TWO

• • • • • • • •

"...report this afternoon."

Gray clouds rolled across the sky, blocking the sizzling rays of the sun but not at all relieving the oppressive heaviness of the tropical air. After a short briefing in the open-air terminal, we were hustled into green Army buses for our trip to the 90th Replacement Battalion on the grounds of the Bien Hoa Army Base. Wire mesh screens covered the windows of our buses to prevent grenades from being tossed through them. Jeeps, armed with M60 machine guns, rode in front of and behind our convoy as we sped through the narrow streets. Shacks made of plywood or pressed sheets of metal beer cans stood on either side of us. Barefoot old men squatted by the side of the road selling cans of gasoline. Exhaust hung in the stagnant air while people went about their business, seemingly oblivious to the latest American convoy. Though images of Vietnam had filled my TV screen for years, the lack of sanitation, the poverty of the shacks, the barefoot men and women, and the mangy water buffaloes stunned me. I wondered how a place so primitive could be so important to the United States. At the same time, after seeing the massive U.S. bases from the air, I wondered if Americans would ever go home.

The ride to the 90th Replacement Battalion did not take long, but it was early evening by the time our buses pulled through its gate. The 90th was a holding facility to which all of us were attached until our individual unit assignments came through. In the officers' section, a dozen brown Army-issue buildings stood together, each with a shingle at the front door to identify its function. Scruffy bushes, clinging to life, grabbed at the sides of the small wooden buildings. Sparse trees, the few that had escaped Army bulldozers, stood near the barbed- wire perimeter.

We attended another briefing in a quonset hut (a steel building shaped like a barrel sawed in half and lying on its side) auditorium, then got our fatigues and malaria pills, and found our lodgings. Sleep could not come soon enough for me. I had gone without it for forty-eight hours. Because we had crossed the International Date Line, my confused inner clock told me it was breakfast time, rather than evening of the current day.

For privacy, the women's quarters were off to the side of the 90th. For protection, a male guard sat at the front door. The building held about a dozen cots separated by plywood partitions. I chose a cot near the front, grabbed soap and a towel from my bag, and took a short path from the back door of the quarters to the "restroom." It consisted of two pit toilets, two sinks and a shower head, all encircled by a stockade fence and home to several lizards and frogs. I stripped and turned on the shower, certain the hot water would ease my aching muscles. In a dribble, icy cold water worked its way out of the rusty head. As I rotated my body under it in a futile effort to freshen myself, I realized that life as I had known it had ended.

Women arriving and departing from Vietnam and taking early morning flights up-country stayed in the quarters. During the night, each time someone entered or left the building, the screen door at the entrance slammed. Artillery hammered in the distance, mosquitoes feasted on me, and diarrhea induced by the malaria pills—given to us without warning of their side-effects— kept me running to the latrine all night. Sleep came in brief, restless spurts.

Except for senior officers, everyone from my flight, women and men, stayed at the 90th for two or three days, waiting for assignments. Gradually, we adjusted to the primitive conditions, the oppressive heat, and each afternoon's monsoon rains. I had no trouble sleeping after I moved to a cot outfitted with mosquito netting at the back of the women's quarters, away from the slamming screen door. I even grew accustomed to the stares of every male officer stationed at or visiting the 90th. Most of the men who walked past me or rode in jeeps said nothing as they stared, though some waved or called. At first the attention surprised and flattered me, then it irritated me, but within hours, I began to ignore it, which was fortunate, because it persisted for the next year.

Nothing was expected of us— not even briefings— so my flightmates and I spent our time in the officers' club and the game room, resting in our quarters, or waiting for the Korean tailors to finish sewing name, rank, and unit patches to our new fatigues. As the men got their assignments and began to leave, we wished each other well and promised to meet at the 90th on our way out of Vietnam in a year's time. No one mentioned what might happen during that year. We seemed to have an unspoken agreement to disregard the war that surrounded us as well as the emotions it induced— a pattern we would follow for our entire tour of duty.

After two days, a green Army sedan took me along with the nine other nurses to the Chief Nurse's office at the United States Army Vietnam Headquarters (USARV) on Long Binh Post, several miles from the 90th. I had been a registered nurse for only twelve months, and I was about to be assigned to a hospital in Vietnam. I felt far more qualified to change places with the driver of the car than to replace a nurse who was completing her tour.

The colonel greeted us pleasantly. She had determined tentative assignments for us, but she asked for our preferences. Thirteen of twenty-six Army hospitals in Vietnam had closed or would be closing during the next year. The ones that were left would carry the burden of care for U.S. forces in-country (in Vietnam). Most of the nurses in my group asked to be sent "up north" to the DMZ (demilitarized zone), or "where the action is." I wanted to request a flight home, but I asked for the 24th Evacuation Hospital because friends at Valley Forge who had been on the staff had recommended it. "OK," said the colonel. "It's here at Long Binh. Get your bags and report this afternoon."

• • • •

CHAPTER THREE

• • • • • • • •

"Oh no, not another new one!"

"So, where would you like to work?" asked the hospital's chief nurse. With trembling hands, I anchored myself to the edge of her desk and leaned forward to respond. "If you put me into the emergency room or operating room," I said slowly, "you'll ship home a wreck. I've done most of my work in internal medicine, and that's where I'd like to be." "Good," she answered, "we have an opening there right now." I was lucky. I had been in the Army long enough to know that I would have been sent wherever she wanted me to go regardless of my request. We were both satisfied with the match.

The 24th Evac, which opened in January, 1967, was one of two evacuation hospitals on Long Binh Post and one of the largest in Vietnam. Though it was designed to hold 328 beds, heavy fighting during the more intense periods of the war kept the census at 400. The hospital housed general medical and surgical wards and served as the referral center for neurosurgery, orthopedics, maxillofacial surgery, ophthamology and otolaryngology. It supported the activities of several infantry units, including the 25th Infantry, the 101st Airborne Division, and the 1st Infantry (Big Red One). But by late 1970, these units had left the region. Most of the patients admitted to the 24th when I arrived in November came from the 1st Cavalry (airmobile) Division or from the Royal Thai Army.

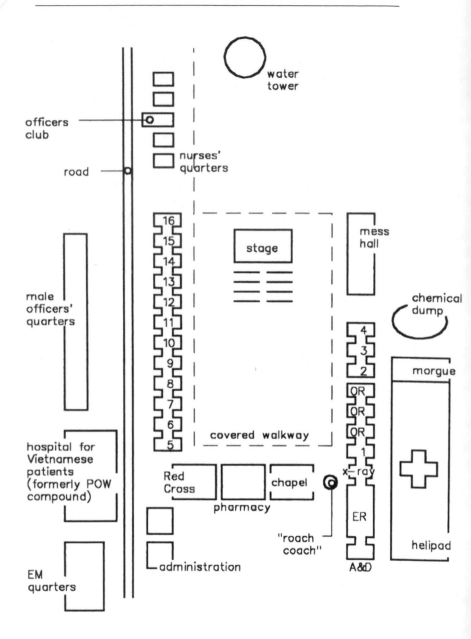

24th EVACUATION HOSPITAL
LONG BINH

A friendly, energetic major took me on a late-afternoon tour. As in most Army hospitals in Vietnam, the patient wards at the 24th were housed in quonset huts that rested on 20 x 80 foot concrete slabs. Along with administrative offices, a mess hall, a chapel and a pharmacy, they surrounded a central quadrangle and were connected to each other by an internal hallway and an outdoor covered walkway. "You'll really appreciate this covered walkway when the rains hit this afternoon," the major assured me. During the six-month monsoon season, which she said was drawing to a close, torrential rains arrived like clockwork late every afternoon and lasted for several hours. The storms, she warned me, would do nothing to clear the oppressive humidity in the air, and the hospital would be left awash in a sea of mud.

At one end of the quadrangle stood a wooden stage on which a small country-and-western USO troupe was performing for approximately fifty patients dressed in blue pajamas. Most of the GIs sat on rows of weather-beaten benches in the hot sun or in wheelchairs, many holding onto poles that carried their IV bottles. Some watched the show from beds that corpsmen had pushed from the wards onto the walkway. USO acts came to the hospital once a week, and the staff tried to get as many GIs as possible to the shows. I would soon discover that the scene in the quadrangle was repeated every night when the back wall of the stage, painted white, became a movie screen. Patients in wheelchairs and beds gathered with off-duty staff to watch anything from a recent release like *Love Story* to a grainy vintage war film like *Sergeant York.* Availability was the only criterion for the choice of movies. At a hospital reunion in 1993, I learned that in early 1969, the roads to and from Long Binh Post were not secure for a full month, and the *Sound of Music* was shown at the 24th over and over, probably to packed houses every night.

The major and I stopped briefly at each of the wards, starting with the side of the hospital devoted to trauma care. The operating rooms, recovery (Ward 1), surgical intensive care unit and general surgical wards (Wards 2,3,4) extended in a straight line from the emergency room, lab and x-ray. When we arrived at the ER, it was quiet. IV bottles, blood pressure cuffs and blood pumps hung on hooks above empty wooden stands, ready to be pressed into service when medevac helicopters landed at the nearby helipad. Patients also came to the 24th Evac in Army ambulances or by jeep. I appreciated how unusual it was for the ER to be quiet when I saw that just about every bed in the intensive care unit and on the surgical wards was occupied. Nurses and corpsmen were busy everywhere, changing IVs and dressings, suctioning patients, taking blood pressures, and talking to the guys. On the wall above each bed hung the unit patch of the soldier who was in the bed.

Across the quadrangle from the operating room was the neurosurgical intensive care unit (Ward 5), for patients who had serious head wounds or spinal cord damage. While other wards had twenty-six beds, the neurosurgical ICU had nineteen beds and four Stryker frames—orbital metal structures designed to shift the position of paraplegic patients from front to back at regular intervals to prevent the development of bedsores. The major said that this ward was generally avoided by staff members who were not assigned to work on it. Taking care of otherwise healthy young men who were missing parts of their brains, or who would never be able move their arms or legs again, was both backbreaking and heartbreaking. GIs with these injuries filled bed after bed on Ward 5. Soldiers with less serious head injuries or back problems went to the adjacent unit, Ward 6. Most of the Ward 6 patients returned to the field after discharge from the 24th.

At the end of Ward 6 stood two plywood cubicles, though they had nothing to do with neurosurgery. They were for hospital staff, men and women who were sick enough to be admitted to the hospital, as well as for other special patients. A nurse told me one occupant had been an American missionary who underwent a radical mastectomy at the 24th because she refused to return to the U.S. for it. Another was an elderly retired nurse, traveling around the world on a steamer, who fractured her clavicle while the ship was moored in Saigon. I looked into the dark cubicles, which had barely enough room for a bed and a side table, and decided I was never going to get sick.

We then stopped at what would be my home for the next year, Wards 7 and 8, the internal medicine unit. With fifty-two patients to care for, the staff barely had time to say a quick hello. The

GIs on Wards 7 and 8 had tropical diseases like malaria, typhus, and dengue fever, as well as asthma, pneumonia, and even heart attacks. Like the other wards, the unit was air-conditioned, but the presence of several large floor fans testified to the ineffectiveness of the air-conditioning against daily 100+ degree temperatures.

Patients recovering from urological and orthopedic surgery were on Wards 9 and 10, while 11 and 12 housed a cast room and physical therapy (PT). By the time we made it to Wards 13 and 14, the unit for convalescing patients, GIs were returning from the USO show just ahead of the rain. The ward's quonset hut roof had the insulating capability of a galvanized washtub, but I was the only one who paid any attention to the din when the monsoon rains hit us with full force. The major merely raised her voice and continued the tour. On Ward 15, the maxillofacial unit, five or six Vietnamese children hurried to greet us. While there had been children on other wards, most were at the 24th for facial reconstruction after boobytrap accidents and burns, or because of birth defects. Within the hospital's alien environment, the kids had created a family for themselves. An older girl held a baby on her hip, while the younger girls and boys clustered around her. The major called each of them by name.

Next to the hospital was the Red Cross building. There, five Red Cross women provided emotional support for the troops. They listened to the GIs' stories, wrote letters for them, organized recreational activities, and coordinated phone calls to the States. Several days a week, they flew to firebases, at the risk of being shot down, to work with troops who could not make it back to Long Binh Post.

Leaving the wards, the major pointed out the sawed-off fifty-gallon drums filled with sand that surrounded each of the wards, the officers' club, and the nurses' quarters. Three or four layers of sand-bags lay on top of the drums. They were supposed to protect against shell fragments and low-velocity missiles, but by late 1970, four years of tropical sun and monsoon rains had eroded them. Looking at the open bags from which the sand oozed, I had no confidence in their ability to stop anything. Despite the hospital's location at the center of the large base, the major told me it was not immune to attack. "The   ammunition dump at Long Binh was hit in '66 and '68," she said, "and that sent mortar and artillery rounds into the hospital com-

pound. In March, 1970, the headquarters building was hit by an enemy rocket, but no one was hurt."

Next, the major took me to the women's quarters, called
hooches—four air-conditioned wooden buildings, not quonset huts.
Each one had ten small private rooms, a tiny community room, and a
restroom with two flush toilets, two sinks, and two metal shower stalls.
As we opened the door to the hooch, the dim light that entered with
us lit only the first few feet of the narrow, damp hallway. We bumped
into an OR nurse on her way out. The major introduced us. "Oh no,"
snarled the nurse, "not another new one! Why are they sending any
more here? After the batch we got last week, what are we going to do
with another one?" I offered to take a plane home, but she did not
appreciate my humor. The door slammed behind her as she stormed
away without another word.

My tour ended at dinnertime, and the major turned me over
to a captain on the hospital staff whom I had known at Valley Forge.
We walked to the mess hall, connected to the rest of the hospital by
the covered walkway. In fact, the only buildings not linked by the
walkway were the morgue, a research unit, the hospital laundry, and
the quarters for male officers and enlisted men (EMs). The mess hall
was a large screened-in building divided into two sections, one for
officers, the other for enlisted men. The captain told me that the crew
served four meals a day to ambulatory patients and staff: breakfast,
lunch, dinner, and a midnight meal. From the moment I arrived for
dinner until I was seated, every pair of eyes in the room rested on me.
Like so many nurses before me, I was an object of curiosity. As a new
American woman in a country where American men outnumbered
us 500 to 1, I became an immediate source of public interest and
discussion. Eventually, I came to realize that everyone stared at me
for another reason: I was a "newbie" with a full tour of duty ahead of
me— something like being the newest inmate in the penal colony.
Long after they all returned to "the world," I would still be in Vietnam.

By the time we finished dinner the rains had stopped, and
we walked to the nurses' quarters where I was to spend the night. I
looked forward to the time alone. My internal clock had not yet adjusted to the time change, and I was overwhelmed by what I had seen—

the hurried pace and noise of the wards, the hundreds of injured and sick soldiers, the omnipresent sandbags. I wondered if I could make it through the next year. More than ever, I questioned my ability to care for the soldiers.

I lay on a bunk in the guestroom. It was like the other rooms in the hooch except for the presence of large aluminum ducts that connected the air-conditioning unit to the rest of the building. Icy water dripped from the large ducts, which took up so much space that regular use of the room was impossible. My bunk had hospital sheets— pale green with large faded brown stains... from the blood that would not wash out. I did not fall asleep for hours.

•　•　•　•

CHAPTER FOUR

• • • • • • • •

"You could probably hitch a ride."

The OR nurse had been right. As she not-so-kindly informed me, a "batch" of nurses from the recently-closed 12th Evacuation Hospital at Cu Chi had arrived at the 24th the week before I did. The temporary increase in nursing staff did not shorten work hours, but it did fill the nurses' quarters. I was to join four of the women from Cu Chi in housing elsewhere on post until rooms opened up for us at the hospital.

A corporal named Tom drove me to the Long Binh housing office, *"Holiday Inn East,"* a small wooden building with a hand-painted *Holiday Inn* logo in front of it. Tom, an outgoing kid from New Jersey, had only fifteen days left in-country. He was more than willing to show me the sprawling forty-eight-square-mile base that he would soon leave.

Long Binh Post was about twenty miles northeast of Saigon in a region once covered by lush rubber plantations. "The Army paid plantation owners $50 a tree before they destroyed them," Tom said. "Now they rent this godforsaken land from the government in Saigon for $700,000 a month. Can you believe it?" When Army bulldozers cleared the land, they removed topsoil along with the trees, and the earth that remained had the consistency of shaved concrete. (Later, I would learn that the military was testing plastic sprays on the Long Binh soil to retard its erosion.) Monsoon rains, without trees or bushes to hold their flow, had carved deep gullies all over the base. Weathered wooden planks bridged these gullies at the entrance to each building and wherever they were too wide to leap over. Long Binh had no color. Most of the buildings were monochromatic brown, dusty during the dry season, dark and damp when it rained. Olive drab trucks and jeeps, like the one in which we rode, blended with olive drab people shrouded in a haze of heat and humidity, dust and exhaust. Many of the jeeps had unit nicknames written just below their windshields, like "Merrill's Marauders." One name came directly from the pages of *Catch 22*—"M&M Enterprises."

Long Binh was one of four major logistic and supply centers for the Army in Vietnam. It was the home of USARV (United States Army Vietnam) headquarters as well as numerous engineering, military police, aviation, quartermaster and other commands, all designed to back up the activity of the GIs in the bush. A honeycomb of paved roads and overhead electrical wires connected the units on base. Housing for the 26,000 Americans assigned to Long Binh in November, 1970—down from 43,000 at the peak of the war--depended on rank. Generals occupied landscaped cottages near the three-story USARV headquarters, field grade officers (majors and above) lived in enclaves of two-bedroom mobile homes, enlisted men stayed in barracks at their units, and a detachment of one hundred WACs (Women's Army Corps) was housed in a compound of five two-story buildings across the road from the 24th Evac.

Twenty-thousand Vietnamese workers entered Long Binh each morning. Most were hoochmaids who did laundry for the Americans. Many were waitresses and cooks employed by the forty clubs on post. Vietnamese aides and orderlies worked in the hospitals and clinics. Vietnamese clerical workers staffed administrative offices and served as translators. We drove past rusting tennis, basketball, and paddleball courts, weed-ridden football and softball fields, and two or three swimming pools, all aboveground with decks for sunning. According to Tom, there were eight pools on base and the most crowded one of the eight was the one near the hospital. "It's close to the PX (Post Exchange) and the soldiers know it's where the nurses swim," he declared, smiling. I was not surprised. I realized from seeing the looks directed at every woman in fatigues that American women in bathing suits would be a real draw.

Joggers were everywhere, apparently unaffected by the jeeps and trucks that stirred up massive clouds of dust around them. The hot sun did not affect the runners, either. "Joggers come out at noon, even in July," said Tom, "the stupid idiots." We rode past an outdoor amphitheater carved into a hollow, the site of Christmas Midnight Mass and the annual Bob Hope Show. "Bob Hope's agenda is supposed to be classified, but everyone knows he comes to Long Binh on Christmas afternoon, probably because of USARV headquarters," Tom explained. "Guys come in from the bush on Christmas Eve. They camp out in the amphitheater and go to the mass and the show. You want to know something? Bob Hope has never spent a night in Vietnam. He flies to Thailand after every show."

The Long Binh housing office assigned me to the only residence for women on the base, about two miles from the 24th Evac. It was one of dozens of buildings that looked just like it on post— two-stories with about twenty private rooms that opened to wooden porches on each floor, a lot like a motel. The bathroom, with sparkling white fixtures and fluorescent lights, was an island of brightness at the center of the drab structure. My building was one of the newer ones on the base, and to this day, the aroma of fresh lumber sends me back to it.

The women from Cu Chi and I were the only nurses to live in the residence. The other occupants were civilian secretaries who worked at USARV headquarters or for the American firms that had built the post in 1966 and were now managing it. On our drive, Tom had pointed out a semi-trailer belonging to one of the companies, a four-firm consortium known as RMK-BRJ. He said that everyone suspected the "J" in "BRJ" was for Johnson—the president's wife. "After all," he insisted, "money has to be the reason we're in Vietnam. There sure as hell can't be any other." Twenty years later, I found out that RMK-BRJ and other American firms had made millions of dollars constructing military facilities and roads in Vietnam, but RMK-BRJ was not connected to the President or his family.

As night fell and the rains stopped, I stood on the porch outside my room, wondering what I had come to. Whatever my image of Vietnam before my arrival, I never could have anticipated the congestion, sheer size and absolute ugliness of the base that now surrounded me. I was in a war where generals lived in cottages, GIs believed we were in-country solely for the money, and the hospital had no room for me. When I asked the clerk at the housing office how I could get to work before dawn each morning, he casually suggested, "You could probably hitch a ride." Meanwhile, the civilian women—in mini-skirts and high-heels— were picked up and taken to work in Army sedans. The sedans were probably air-conditioned.

• • • •

CHAPTER FIVE

• • • • • • • •

"I'd have to get better to die."

The young sandy-haired soldier lay motionless in bed. As I approached him, he turned his head to me and gave me a weak smile. Illness clouded his blue eyes. The head nurse had asked me to put an IV in him, something I had never done. Though he had the prominent veins of any nineteen-year-old male, I missed them twice. I felt terrible, but with lots of "ma'ams" and a soft smile, he encouraged me to keep trying. He probably would have let me turn both of his arms into pin cushions without complaint. That young GI was my introduction to the patients at the 24th Evac.

Earlier that morning, the staff had welcomed me to Wards 7 and 8. In a small ceremony, the ward NCO (sergeant) added my name to the DEROS chart. DEROS, "Date Eligible for Return from OverSeas," was the day I could go home. In World War II and Korea, military personnel stayed overseas until the war's end, but in Vietnam, Marines stayed for thirteen months while Army and Navy tours were twelve— "364 days and a wake-up." From the moment our feet touched Asian soil, we began a countdown, and at any point during the next year, each one of us—women, men, infantry or support troops— knew exactly how many days we had left in-country. Even if I had wanted to forget, the doctors and corpsmen on the ward would not have let me. They cheered loudly when, next to my name, the sergeant wrote in my DEROS date of November 15th as well as my 359 days left in country. Others' numbers ranged from nine to 330.

The unit held fifty-two beds on two wards, including eight for intensive care patients. The beds and small tables between them filled the long quonset huts, leaving little room to maneuver around the patients. Linoleum covered the cement-slab floors; the overhead lights were fluorescent. A short hallway connected the two wards. Cabinets for equipment, shelves for IV fluids and chart racks lined one wall of it. Opposite them were two overstuffed, green vinyl armchairs. The chairs were the heart as well as the hub of the unit. When soldiers arrived on the wards from the bush (the jungle), they sat in them to be admitted. During less hectic periods, nurses, doctors, and corpsmen slumped in them to rest, and because our mail was delivered to the ward, we often read our letters from "the world" in them. Next to the chairs was the entrance to a large restroom that held two showers, sinks, and several flush toilets.

The staff came from all regions of the United States and a wide variety of educational backgrounds. The chief of medicine was the only physician who had been drafted after completing his residency, just as he was to begin private practice. (Doctors could be drafted until they were thirty-five.) He and the other three doctors— drafted during their residency programs— were getting intensive on-the-job training in tropical medicine. The head nurse, a captain, had been on active duty two years longer than I. She managed the unit. A sergeant wardmaster supervised the corpsmen and maintained supplies. Five staff nurses, all of us recent graduates of nursing school who had come into the Army through the student nurse program, and eight corpsmen, all draftees, cared for the patients twelve-and-a-half hours a day, six days a week. Everyone worked a week of days, had a single day off, shifted to a week of nights and then back to days. The Vietnamese aide, Son Dinh Nguyen, was the only person who expected to be on the ward in a year's time. Everyone else would be home.

The unit's daily schedule remained the same for the year I was there. Every morning, the doctors discharged ten or twelve GIs to return to the bush or to the large convalescent center at Cam Ranh Bay, to Japan or the States. By late afternoon, their beds were filled by soldiers who had waited at firebases (semi-permanent camps in the bush) until an available truck, jeep, or helicopter could bring them to Long Binh. After being seen in the 24th Evac's medical clinic, they came to the ward dressed in dirty fatigues and muddy boots, carrying admission papers from the clinic. Emaciated and exhausted from months in the bush, with temperatures ranging anywhere from 103 to 106 degrees, they wanted only to lie down and feel better. In listless voices, one after another told us, "I'd have to get better to die." We took a short history and vital signs—pulse, respirations, blood pressure, temperature—on each GI while he sat in one of the big green armchairs. We drew blood and started appropriate medications. Then a corpsman helped the soldier into clean blue pajamas, gave him a small bag of personal hygiene items supplied by the Red Cross, and took him to his long-awaited bed. Despite feeling miserable, the guys were happy to be out of the jungle and in the hospital looking at American women — they called us "round eyes." The majority were enlisted men from the 1st Cavalry (airmobile) Division. Most were infantry soldiers, or "grunts." They had come from urban streets and country roads all over America. Draft deferments had just not been in the cards for them. I was only twenty-three myself, but I felt old around our patients. They were like big kids. Most were eighteen or nineteen years old. Many had not yet started to shave.

Four months of civilian experience in internal medicine and six months as a pediatric nurse at Valley Forge General Hospital hardly prepared me for the complexity of illnesses I saw on Wards 7 and 8. The most common admission diagnosis was "FUO," fever of unknown origin. In many cases, it took days for blood work—some of which was done in Japan— to document the cause of a soldier's fever. Until we got the lab results, we did not know if he had one of two different kinds of malaria, blackwater fever, typhus, dengue fever, or septicemia (blood poisoning). Just about everyone had dysentery, skin rashes and sores. Some patients had gastrointestinal bleeds or pneumonia. Soldiers with asthma came to us in severe respiratory distress. Cardiac problems were not unusual. We even had patients who needed rabies shots because wild monkeys they adopted as pets had bitten them and run off into the jungle.

Most of our patients had either vivax or falciparum malaria, caused by parasites in the blood and characterized by three-stage attacks called paroxysms. In the "cold stage" a soldier shivered and shook. No number of blankets kept him warm. After an hour of shivering, he entered the "hot stage." His temperature spiked, often close to 106 degrees. We put him in a tepid shower, gave him an alcohol sponge bath or placed him on a cooling blanket, all in an effort to reduce his fever. After about two hours, as suddenly as it had started, the "hot stage" came to an end. The soldier broke into a profuse sweat, and his temperature plummeted to normal. We changed his soaking wet bed and moved the cooling unit to yet another patient who was just entering the hot stage. Unfortunately, because the two different malarias called for different medications, we had to wait for lab verification to start the appropriate drugs. We were always relieved when the diagnosis came through, and we could start the correct treatment.

Between paroxysms, soldiers with malaria were exhausted but otherwise felt fine. Vivax paroxysms occurred every other day. Falcip paroxysms were irregular and longer, and they caused higher temperatures. Falcip malaria could cause vomiting, diarrhea and gastrointestinal bleeds. It was more dangerous than vivax because the parasites blocked capillaries in vital organs. If they settled in the brain (cerebral malaria), the soldier went into a coma. Without a ten-day course of IV quinine, he died.

Because its pattern was so crazy, I was sure our patients with malaria would want to know why they felt good one day and miserable the next. So if we had a quiet afternoon, I made nursing rounds to talk to them about the disease, describing the life cycle of the parasite and what it did to blood vessels. One afternoon, I spoke to two young privates in adjoining beds who had vivax malaria. One of them had heard my detailed explanation the previous day, and I asked him to explain the disease to his buddy, who was new to the ward. The young GI, happy to accomodate me, sat on the edge of his bed, threw his foot across his knee, leaned forward earnestly and said quite simply, "These bugs, they get into your body and do a job on you." From then on, I shortened my explanation!

All of our patients from the Royal Thai Army had blackwater fever, a severe complication of falciparum malaria. They had ex-

tremely high temperatures— a Thai soldier came to the emergency
room one night with a temperature of 107.2— and an excess of cir-
culating hemoglobin from the blood cells destroyed by the malaria
parasites. The excreted hemoglobin turned their urine very dark, almost black. Sometimes, their kidneys could not handle the heavy load
of hemoglobin, and they stopped functioning. If this happened, we
sent the patient to the Third Field Hospital in Saigon for dialysis (ar-
tificial kidney). Most of the Thai soldiers did not need dialysis, but
they were with us for up to a month because they were so sick. One
morning on Ward 7, report had just started when a disoriented soldier decided he had had enough of the 24th Evac. He stood up on his
bed and shouted at the top of his voice, "Go Bangkok!" Then he ripped
out his IV and Foley catheter, jumped over the foot of the bed and
ran out the back door of the ward trailing blood, two corpsmen in
hot pursuit. They brought him back, and he calmed down and recovered. I hope he made it to Bangkok.

Our sickest patients came to us from the emergency
room, not the clinic. They had cerebral malaria, encephalitis, men-
ingitis, or fulminant hepatitis (a sudden, intense onset of the disease).

Because they went to the States soon after they regained consciousness, we never knew if they recovered. However, we were able
find out what happened to one of our more memorable patients, Tom
Smith, a GI with severe encephalitis. No one thought he would survive, but after a week in a coma he showed signs of consciousness and
some slight muscle control. Tom made steady but very slow progress
during the next few weeks. His speech came back gradually, and so
did his ability to walk. The first time he stood and took a few hesitant
steps away from his bed, he looked like a six-foot-four toddler. Lurch-
ing around the ward, he stared at everything with wide-open eyes,
not comprehending where he was or what had happened to him. He
continued to improve in every respect and was evacuated to the States,
not fully recovered but well on his way. A day after he left us, one of
the nurses found Tom's wallet on the ward and sent it to his family.
Tom himself wrote back after several months to thank us for our care
and to let us know he was doing OK. He said he had no memory of
his time in the hospital and asked us to tell him what had occurred.

After that, whenever a patient with a neurological problem had that wide-eyed appearance, we called it the "Tom Smith look."

The recovery of another comatose patient brought all of us to tears. Tony had severe liver damage from fulminant hepatitis. As with Tom, we held out little hope for his recovery. But one morning, a nurse realized he had responded slightly to her care. Elated, she told the doctor when he began his rounds. The doctor did not believe her. "You're imagining it," he said, but he agreed to do an exam. We stood around his bed to watch, our own eyes filling, as Tony voluntarily blinked his eyes at the doctor's command. He literally had come back from the dead. He went on to a full recovery before we sent him home.

Soldiers scheduled for evacuation began to get excited when the manifest arrived on the ward with their names posted for the next day's flight to the States. They put together their few possessions to which we attached luggage tags marked with a military flight number and destination in the U.S. None of them slept the night before departure. At dawn, they boarded buses to Ton Son Nhut Airbase in Saigon. Some buses were outfitted for stretchers, others had seats. In Saigon, they boarded C-130 transport planes. Patients who required intensive care went to Saigon by helicopter where they were moved to specially-equipped Air Force evacuation flights. Sometime during the night before they left the 24th, Air Force flight nurses phoned us for verbal reports on the soldiers' conditions. Sending the GIs back to "the world" with a real chance to live was the highlight of the year for all of us.

After just a few weeks of working on Ward 7 and 8, I began to believe that the Army's only health prerequisite for service in Vietnam was a pulse. Some of our patients should never have been in-country. Many had asthma, and several GIs with cardiac valve problems were sent to the war despite the unavailability of open-heart surgery in Vietnam. We evacuated one GI to the Philippines for an emergency heart operation, but two more died at the 24th before we could send them out.

We did care for non-surgical cardiac patients, and during the summer of '71, we opened a cardiac care unit (CCU) with four state-of-the-art monitors. Within days, we admitted Sgt. Cook. He had come to the emergency room in cardiac arrest after a major heart attack. An ER doctor tried to resuscitate him for forty-five minutes before he called off the effort. Just as the doctor stopped pumping his chest, Sgt. Cook reached up and pulled the breathing tube from his throat. He began a very slow recovery in the CCU despite having a second heart attack while he was with us.

Sgt. Cook became everyone's friend. He freely shared his near-death experiences and convinced us his thick white hair had been dark before his heart attack. We were never able to find out if he was kidding. On doctor's orders, he kept a volleyball at the foot of his bed where he gently rolled it around with his feet to keep the blood flowing in his legs. One hectic day, the nursing supervisor, a major, arrived on the ward to berate the charge nurse for some insignificant infraction. The major, who was always on us about something, chose Jan Hyche, probably the most dedicated nurse on the unit, as her "victim of the day." Jan never walked, she ran. Tendrils of sandy hair frequently worked their way out of her ponytail. "They should fit us all with Foley catheters and leg bags," she often said. "That way we wouldn't have to take time out to go to the bathroom." Watching the supervisor treat Jan so vilely was more than Sgt. Cook could take. He reached down to his feet, picked up his volleyball and hurled it at the major's head. It narrowly missed its target, brushing her hair as it flew by. She whirled around in anger looking for the source of the missile, only to see a group of patients lying quietly in bed. Lecture forgotten, she stormed off the ward.

Sgt. Cook was not unique. The soldiers would have done anything for us and we for them. One night, the ward was unusually quiet as Jan, again the nurse on duty, sat charting in dim light at the nurses' desk. Glancing at the patient in the bed opposite the desk, she saw he was watching two giant cockroaches crawling down the wall towards him. He had an IV in each arm, so he was powerless to stop their approach. Jan quietly folded a paper and carefully approached his bed. She planned her attack to avoid waking the other patients. "I took a swing at them with my paper," Jan said, "and both roaches flew right into my face. I let out a blood-curdling scream." Every patient who was not unconscious jumped out of his bed, ready to defend her. After Jan reassured them she was OK, everyone laughed and went back to sleep. The cockroaches got away.

We rarely had celebrity visitors. Miss America and her court were the only ones to visit our unit during the year I was there. They greeted every patient on the ward, and the GIs loved it. USO troupes, who came to the hospital regularly, performed in the quadrangle, and Bob Hope's show was in the large post amphitheater. On Christmas afternoon, 1970, twenty-one patients, two doctors, one nurse and several corpsmen from Wards 7 and 8 went to the production, not quite believing they would be part of something they had watched on TV year after year. The temperature was 104 degrees, and there was no shade to be found anywhere near the amphitheater. The corpsmen carried large plastic garbage bags filled with towels soaked in cold water for the patients to put on their heads and necks. Everyone returned with happy memories and sunburned faces.

Generals came to the wards on Sundays. Surrounded by aides, they went bed to bed, pinning Purple Heart medals (for injuries during wartime) to pajamas and chatting with soldiers from their units. One Sunday, a general almost suffered a cardiac arrest himself. One of our patients was a sailor. As the general went through the ward, the sailor hid his face behind a newspaper he was reading until the general stopped at the adjoining bed. Casually, the seaman lowered the paper to reveal a full beard. The startled commander took a moment to realize he was looking at someone from the only branch of service that allowed beards. Everyone on the ward, particularly the patients, enjoyed seeing the shock on the general's face. He and his entourage quickly moved on to the next "Army-occupied" bed.

Early one morning, another general endeared himself to us when he arrived on the ward as a concerned parent. The night nurse had just started giving us her report. Two corpsmen and I listened to it seated on a gurney (stretcher on wheels) we had pushed up against the nurses' desk. Suddenly, the corpsman sitting at the end of the gurney felt a light tap on his shoulder. When he turned his head, he found himself looking directly at a star on a fatigue collar. Shouting "YES SIR!" he pushed the gurney back from the desk, toppling the three of us to the floor. The general helped us up and told us to relax. He had come to visit his son, who was one of our patients. He merely wanted to know where his son's bed was. The general had come by

himself. He pulled up a chair next to his son's bed and had a quiet
twenty-minute visit with him.

Once, we had a general as a patient. Senior officers and any
U.S. officials usually went to the Third Field Hospital in Saigon. But
one morning, the hospital commander told us a two-star general was
coming in for a diagnostic proctoscopy. He was to encounter the "silver bullet" —the long chrome instrument used for intestinal exami-
nations. Dysentery was so common among our patients that a staff
doctor, assisted by a corpsman, did seven or eight proctoscopies daily.
On orders from above, however, the general's proctoscopy was to be
done by the chief of medicine, who had not done one since he arrived in Vietnam, assisted by the sergeant wardmaster, a nervous little
man who had never even watched one done. The panicked sergeant
hurriedly assembled the equipment while he took a crash course on
what to do from the corpsmen. Meanwhile, a bevy of administrative
staff members ushered the unsuspecting general onto the ward. One
of our corpsmen, a big kid from Philadelphia, could not believe the
display of military protocol at the expense of patient care. John threw
himself into one of the green vinyl armchairs and announced to anyone who would listen, "If I look up that general's asshole and I see
two stars, *then and only then*, will I salute." Fortunately, the general,
who was otherwise occupied, did not hear him.

Our only true VIP was a released POW, an Army sergeant,
whom we admitted in October, 1971. The Viet Cong captured him in
August, 1969, when he was cut off from his platoon during an ambush. Soon after his capture, he wrote a letter that made its way to
U.S. authorities. Despite it, the Army told his parents that their son
was probably dead. His captors dragged him through much of South
Vietnam and into the Cambodian highlands. When he was not serving them, they tied him by a short rope to a stake in the ground. Once
a day he ate scraps mixed with rice. After twenty-seven torturous
months, the Viet Cong unexpectedly gave him a map and a safe-con-
duct pass and pointed him down a road. Nine miles later, he walked
into an encampment of U.S. Army soldiers. Within the hour, he was
with us at the 24th Evacuation Hospital.

Looking considerably older than his twenty-one years, the
sergeant was a broken young man. Vitamin deficiency from his poor

diet had caused his hair to fall out. Sores covered his skin. Blood and pus oozed from the ones on his feet. Many teeth were gone. Some had fallen victim to the butt of his captor's gun, others to his poor diet. His arm, broken before capture, had never been set and had healed in a permanently flexed position. His injured right eye was almost blind. He had malaria. He never thought he would be freed and said the hardest part of his ordeal was looking up from the jungle to see U.S. planes overhead and out of reach. He remembered a helicopter pilot spotting him, waving, and flying away just before he was captured. He thought his release was a dream. Afraid to sleep for fear he would wake up in the jungle, he spent the entire first night talking about his captivity and asking about "the world." For two years, his only news had come from Radio Hanoi. He was well aware of the anti-war movement, and when I told him I had graduated from Columbia University, he recognized it as the school where Mark Rudd had founded the Students for a Democratic Society (SDS), an anarchistic anti-war group. He was not with us for long. By the time he was evacuated to the States for reconstructive surgery on his arm, he had shown considerable improvement on the strength of a good diet, vitamin supplements, and medications.

On Wards 7 and 8, physicians and nurses made patient rounds every morning, but the doctors soon left to staff the hospital's medical clinic the rest of the day. Nurses managed patient care on the ward. Most of the time, nurses and doctors worked well together. Twice, however, our head nurses engaged in major confrontations with the doctors over patient care. The first altercation occurred when I had been on the staff for only a few weeks. A young Latino corporal who needed to have a catheter inserted in an arm vein and threaded towards his shoulder— an uncomfortable procedure— had a complication that made it worse. A partial obstruction in his vein made passage of the catheter impossible. Each time the doctor tried to push the catheter through the vein, the kid screamed out in Spanish. The doctor tried repeatedly without success. Before long, all the doctors crowded around the bed, while the rest of the patients on the ward watched anxiously. In turn, each physician insisted he could succeed and attacked the vein. The GI alternated between shrieking and sobbing. After the third doctor's futile attempts, the head nurse could stand it no longer. She called them aside and angrily instructed them, "Get off the ward until you can treat patients like human beings!" The doctors were surprised, but they turned to leave— all but one. The lone holdout sullenly challenged, "What makes you think it's your ward?" Without a second's hesitation, she fired back, "Because I spend a hell of a lot more time here than you. Now, get out of here!" He left. She then called a surgeon to insert the catheter above the obstruction. When it was over, she sat down at the nurses' desk, covered her face with her hands and cried.

Toward the end of my tour, our head nurse, Judy Thoesen, was in a similar position, between physician and patient. Taking advantage of a slow afternoon, Judy had gone to her room for a short break. A staff nurse called her to return immediately to the ward. One of our patients had empyema (pus around a lung). Doctors had put in a chest tube to drain it. Unfortunately, the GI's other lung collapsed as a doctor was putting an IV into his subclavian vein. "When I got back to the ward," Judy said, "an internist was trying to get the kid stabilized. He was getting nowhere, and he wouldn't call anyone else. We needed a surgeon right away. We had only one phone on the ward and some poor patient was using it. I remember screaming to the poor kid, 'Get off that phone RIGHT NOW!' He dropped it. I called the OR and said, 'I need anesthesia right now, and I need a surgeon right now.' The kid was crunching fast. Thank God, we got him stabilized. We had a real mix of doctors and nurses. Most of them gave their all. But there was no quality assurance, so you hoped the good staff people would compensate for the bad."

There was little interaction between staff who worked on the different units in the hospital. Standing in our central hallway, we could see from Ward 5 to Ward 14, yet no one made an effort to visit other wards. Staff on the medical units rarely ventured across the quadrangle to the surgical wards. None of us had the time or energy to explore. We also suffered from emotional overload. No one in medicine wanted to see what came through the ER door. We had our hands full with our own brand of casualties.

In many ways, those of us who worked in internal medicine had an advantage. Our patients were overwhelmingly sick, but war had not mutilated them. Most of the GIs recovered while they were with us. We got to know them because they stayed with us for extended periods of time. But knowing them was also a disadvantage: our patients returned to the war. Sending them back to danger ran counter to the heart and soul of nursing. It was the most difficult thing we were called on to do. Yet we did it, and we never talked about it or its effect on us. As weeks turned into months on Wards 7 and 8, I became expert at suppressing my emotions. It was the only way I could send kids back to a war that became more meaningless as each day passed. Smothering my feelings, I put in my time, counted the days until I could go home, and did the best job I could. At a 24th Evac reunion more than twenty years later, I learned that other nurses had done the same to survive. Judy Thoesen remembered, "There was no way to vent feelings about what was happening to the guys, so you stayed isolated. A person could get involved with a patient up to a point. But you had to keep some distance, you had to think about yourself. The ones who didn't got really screwed up. Looking back now I think, 'Why didn't I do more? When it was Christmas and I was off, why didn't I go visit the GIs?' But I had to get away, I had to keep my own sanity, I had to separate myself."

One young soldier broke through my wall and remains with me today. Jim was a gawky eighteen-year-old admitted to the ward with vivax malaria. He was on IV fluids. Because more than half the patients were on IVs at any point in time, we put a strip of tape marked with hourly increments on the side of each IV bottle to monitor the progress of the fluids. One night when I made rounds, I lifted my flashlight to Jim's bottle. At the top of the tape, he had written, "Hi Mary!" He lay asleep below it. After Jim returned to the bush, he sent me chatty letters about his unit and how he hated what he was doing.

Jim returned to the hospital in a month with another attack of vivax, his six-foot frame carrying no more than 120 pounds. He recovered, was discharged and sent back to the jungle. He continued to write to me. Several months later, I was caring for a patient when I looked up to see him being wheeled onto the ward yet again. As he rolled by on the gurney, he weakly flashed me a "thumbs up" sign. Jim thought he had his ticket home. After three attacks of malaria, soldiers usually were evacuated. However, Jim did not know the evacuation policy specified that the GI had to have three attacks of the same kind of malaria. Jim's third case was falciparum malaria. He recovered, but when he returned to his unit, he was very weak. I never heard from him again. Fifteen years later, on my first visit to the Vietnam Veterans Memorial (the Wall), his was the first name I looked for. Happily, it was not there. Today, I'd like to go back in time to argue his case, to damn the policy, and to send him home.

Reflecting on my year at the 24th Evacuation Hospital, images flick across my mind like the frames of a film. I see running, constant running, and I see smiles. I see us in olive drab fatigues, the most comfortable and functional nursing uniforms ever made. (For months after my return to stateside nursing, I futilely reached to my shoulder for the tourniquet, scissors, clamp, and pen I knew belonged in the fatigue shoulder pocket.) I see endless IVs. I see the ward decorated for Christmas with construction paper stockings, angel hair, tinsel and wreaths. (We won the ward decorating contest that year!) I see nurses and corpsmen painting ward cabinets bright yellow and red (the only colors we could scrounge from supply). I see us sitting around on slow nights, talking about what we plan to do when we get back to "the world" (have a hamburger, drive a car). I see GIs in blue pajamas sitting on their beds, talking about home, women, and sports (never the war). I see patients going out to the quadrangle in wheelchairs to catch the nightly movie. (Jan called it the "drive-in theater.") I see old suction machines juryrigged to work. I see green portable oxygen tanks tightly secured so that we do not have to worry about one accidentally falling, cracking open, and racing around the ward like a torpedo. I see corpsmen using all of their strength to crack the valves open in emergencies, so no patient would be deprived of oxygen. I see gecko lizards at night piled above the door to the ward, struggling to get close to the naked light bulb. (We had to open the door quickly and run in with our collars held close to our necks, hoping the geckos would not fall into our shirts.) I see the paper-towel dispenser from Green Bay, Wisconsin. (I wonder if the people in Green Bay knew I thought about them every time I saw it.) I see the proud, smiling face of a young soldier as I pin on the Purple Heart medal he earned with his body. (He wanted no officer but me to do it!) I see some of our Vietnamese patients, the little babies with devoted mothers who came to care for them, and the old man with bubonic plague.

(The "Black Death" of the Middle Ages, not uncommon in Vietnam of 1971.) I see lots of life and some death, all of it unnecessary. I see face after face - black, brown, and white - returned to health, only to leave us wondering if they would be the last GIs killed in Vietnam.

• • • •

CHAPTER SIX

• • • • • • •

"If you miss it this time, I'm going to be dead."

"Hi! How y'all doin'?" came the greeting from the doorway. At the sound of the voice, I stopped shoving my clothes into drawers and turned to meet my new neighbor, Stephanie Genthon. Exactly one month after arriving at the 24th Evac, temporary quarters and pre-dawn hitchhiking were behind me! Now, as a resident of hooch #3, I would roll out of bed after an extra half-hour's sleep to make my way down the covered walkway to Wards 7 and 8.

Stephanie worked in the emergency room. She had returned to her room for a short nap, and seeing my open door, she stopped in to welcome me to the hooch. She was shorter than I, with long sandy-blond hair pulled back into a low ponytail. Her engaging smile and deep Southern drawl conveyed the warmth of her native Mississippi. She introduced me to the hoochmaids (mamasans) who would be doing my laundry and filled me in on hooch routines like the use of the phone and where to post messages. Then she tactfully suggested that I might want to eat lunch elsewhere because every day at noon, the mamasans cooked their lunch on a hot plate in the community room. The seasoning they used was made from the residue of decaying fish. "It's called *nuoc mam*," Stephanie said. "I've heard it doesn't taste so bad, but the odor is so foul, I haven't gotten close enough to try it. The smell fills the whole hooch."

Two other nurses stopped by to say hello. As we chatted, Stephanie realized the background sound of churning helicopter blades had grown louder. A quick look revealed a flurry of activity at the helipad. Out went her cigarette, on went her boots. Running out the door, she called "good-bye!" I did not see her for three days.

• • • •

Like me, Stephanie had entered the military through the Army Student Nurse Program. Also like me, she had not wanted to come to Vietnam. When I met her, she had been at the 24th Evacuation Hospital for six months. "I paid attention to combat nursing courses during basic training because being in the military meant understanding the casualties of war," she told me twenty years later. "But I knew I was never going to the war itself." When orders arrived, she tried unsuccessfully to get them changed. In June,1970, a year after graduating from an Alabama nursing school, she flew to Vietnam on an infantry transport. She was twenty-one years old.

"Every time the plane stopped to refuel," she remembered, "I expected an officer would come onboard to announce the war was over, and I could go home." It did not happen. When the transport eventually landed at a deserted runway in Saigon, no one knew where to send Stephanie, the only woman on the flight. A duty sergeant made several phone calls before he instructed her to take an Army bus marked with a red stripe. He told her to transfer at the end of the line to one with a blue stripe for her trip to USARV Headquarters. At the last stop, the blue one was nowhere in sight. Stephanie was reluctant to leave the security of her bus, but in broken English, the Vietnamese driver told her to cross the road and take the one with the yellow stripe. "No one else talked to me or offered to help me," she said. "So I took my suitcases and staggered across the dirt road in my high heels. There I was, in the middle of a war I didn't want to be in after a twenty-six- hour flight, taking the advice of a Vietnamese driver." Eventually, after moving her suitcases "on and off every damn bus they had," Stephanie ended up at Ton Son Nhut Air Base where she caught a convoy to Long Binh. "They literally dropped me at the side of the road near the gate," she remembered. "The guard at the gate repeated what I had heard all day, 'What are you doing here? Nurses don't come here.' I was sick and tired of hearing it. But he called an MP who took me to the Chief Nurse, a colonel, at USARV Headquarters."

"By the time I hit her office, I was really losing it," Stephanie recalled. She had come 8,000 miles, and had taken six hours to travel the final twenty. She had not slept for two days. "I've had trouble my entire adult life with ankle swelling," she said, "but my ankles have never been as big as they were that day." The colonel took her by the hand, led her to a chair, and propped her feet on another chair. She gave Stephanie a Coke and apologized for what had happened to her. Then she said, "After all you've been through, you don't need to go anywhere else. I'm sending you to the 24th Evac, right here at Long Binh."

The chief nurse at the hospital assigned Stephanie to the surgical intensive care unit (Ward 2) because she had worked for six months in an ICU at Madigan General Hospital in Tacoma, Washington. Before Madigan, Stephanie had never seen an ICU, nor had she seen a patient die. She was not ready for the 24th. Her first day on duty, watching the staff in action, she thought, "I can't do this. I don't know what I'm doing." Within weeks, she made the adjustment.

Even nurses with considerably more experience than Stephanie were unprepared for what they faced in Vietnam. The shattered bodies of U.S. soldiers came directly from the field to Army hospitals. Weapons were designed not only to kill, but to maim and mutilate. Bullets from high-velocity assault rifles (M-16s and AK-47s) did not travel straight through bodies. They ricocheted through their victims, tearing at muscle, bone and organs along their irregular paths. One round simultaneously could perforate a colon, small intestine, duodenum, pancreas, and stomach. It could shred a liver and sever major blood vessels. Grenades peppered bodies with fragments of shrapnel (pieces of metal or glass) that permeated muscle and organs. Claymore mines and booby traps amputated arms and legs, severed spinal cords, and blinded thousands of GIs. In the OR at the 24th, it was not unusual for a general surgeon, an orthopedic surgeon, and a neurosurgeon to operate on the same patient at the same time. "The operating theaters were separated by rolling screens," a surgeon told me at the hospital reunion in 1993. "And I will never forget the sight of blood from separate cases mixing on the floor under our feet."

"Friendly" fire caused the worst injuries. American soldiers hit by U.S. artillery arrived burned beyond recognition. So did casualties of helicopter crashes and napalm victims. The war raised emergency care to a "state of the art" level. Many critical care measures were introduced and refined in the ten-year carnage of the Vietnam War. Patients who would have died in previous wars made it to military hospitals and lived. In 1971, a Walter Reed Army Insitute of Research study discovered that it took an average of only eighteen minutes for a soldier with a priority injury to go directly from the field to the 24th Evac's operating room.[1]

The surgical intensive care unit had twenty-one beds. The average census was seventeen GIs, "so damn sick and all filled with holes," Stephanie said. On the day shift, she worked with several nurses; most nights she worked with a single corpsman. "The routine was always the same," she explained. "The two of us filled a dressing cart with supplies, and went bed-to-bed, changing dressings and taking care of Foley catheters. There were no curtains or privacy of any kind. The guys laid their wounds out to be squirted and rinsed, dabbed and dressed four times a day."

Stephanie remembers a continuous procession of young faces without names, many soldiers who died, and ones who barely made it out of Vietnam alive. She recalls one GI whose femoral artery (main artery to the leg) was severed by shrapnel. Surgeons patched the vessel with a graft. "We couldn't send him home until he had been with us for a full two weeks," said Stephanie, "to make sure the graft wouldn't tear open in transit." One hour before the soldier was to leave in an evacuation helicopter, the graft broke open. He immediately went to the operating room for a repair. Two weeks later, the graft ruptured again. Stephanie finally put him on a flight after six weeks and three operations, hoping his patched vessel would survive the trip. "Getting him on the plane was the highlight of my year," she said, and added, "I hope he didn't blow in the air."

Another patient's femoral graft broke just before his scheduled evacuation. Within seconds, bright red blood saturated his sheets.

Stephanie tried twice without luck to start an IV in him. Before her eyes, the GI was turning gray. As she got ready to stick him a third time, he looked up at her and said, "Stephanie, if you miss it this time, I'm going to be dead." "Well," she thought, "I have to do something." She climbed up on him, sat on his abdomen to put pressure on the wound, and got "the damn IV into him." She sent the corpsman for blood. When he returned with it, Stephanie was still sitting on the soldier. "He was gonna die if I didn't," she said simply. He recovered.

One quadriplegic patient remained on Ward 2 while the U.S. Congress worked to get him home. "The only way he could breathe was with a volume ventilator [a machine that delivers a fixed amount of air to the lung]," Stephanie explained. "Unfortunately, to be air-evac'd, patients had to be on pressure ventilators [which depended on pressure, not volume, to determine the amount of air delivered to the lungs]." After two months, a congressional mandate outfitted a plane with the appropriate equipment, and the GI went home.

In a mass-cal (mass casualty), a busy Ward 2 became chaotic. "The ER and OR would push for hours," recalled Stephanie. "As they were beginning to quiet down, we'd get rev'd up because they'd be sending patients to us. We'd have to ship guys to Wards 3 and 4, guys we weren't really ready to send, but we had to make room." The surgical intensive care unit had all the equipment available in 1970, but Stephanie remembers running out of it. "There were times when four patients needed ventilators and the unit had three. A decision had to be made about who would use them," she said. There were times when there were few clean sheets, and the corpsmen could change only the dirtiest beds. "There were just so many guys," Stephanie said. "One night we ran out of morphine. We also ran out of antibiotics, not for long stretches, but for a day or two."

Death came in spells. "One group of GIs would come in torn apart and they would all die," she remembered. "Another group might arrive together and they would all live." On Stephanie's worst night, seven patients died. She and a corpsman put them into body bags and left them outside the back door of the ward. She, herself, never called the morgue. Instead, she asked the corpsman to do it. Nor did she go outside to make sure they had been picked up. She could not have handled it. "It was always somebody's son or boyfriend," she said. "They were so nice, so young, and so scared, it made it twice as hard to see them die." Sometimes it was harder for the staff to care for soldiers who did not die immediately— the GIs who were still under attack in their dreams, or those who died after days of misery.

Stephanie felt the patients glorified the nurses, probably because they depended on them so much. "In their eyes we became greater than we were," she explained. "We were their wives, mothers, sisters, girlfriends. We had to be everything." She remembers writing letters to mothers and girlfriends and receiving answers from some families. "Only once," she said, "in all the months I spent in the ICU, did I have a patient who was critical and ugly to me. The rest of the patients chewed him out."

The Ward 2 staff sometimes found themselves thinking of severely-wounded patients as fortunate. Joanne Kane Halcomb, the nurse who oriented Stephanie to the ICU, described these feelings in a letter to her parents:

. . . We have patients who have lost nothing but a few months of living while they're in a hospital and an eye. Here we think someone is lucky if all he's lost is an eye. But think of what it would be like to lose an eye. We have a sweetheart right now, cute as anything, who loves folk music. He plays the guitar. He lost his right arm last week—no more guitar. But we think of him as lucky. . .

Nurses, doctors, and corpsmen on Ward 2 became family to each other. Crazy antics were commonplace. "Sometimes we got so rowdy at night, we woke up the patients and then they joined us in the fun," Stephanie said. But beneath the good-natured teasing lay a sadness that could not be expressed and an anger that had to be concealed. No one spoke about the war. "The patients needed to believe in what they were doing," explained Stephanie. "It was the glue that held them together. If they lost that, it would all be over. We were just taking care of sick people. They were out there fighting. How could we be critical of the war? They needed to believe that what they did was worthwhile." After nine months, however, the pressure got to her. She began to verbalize that she did not understand why so many guys were dying. Afraid she would let loose in front of the soldiers, she requested a transfer from the ICU.

Stephanie probably was one of very few nurses in Vietnam who went to the emergency room for relief. "At least you didn't have to get to know the guys," she said. The ER pace was so fast, the soldiers had such urgent physical needs, there was no time to develop a relationship with them. But even for Stephanie, who was accustomed to the ICU, mass-cals in the ER required adjustment. "At first I didn't think I could do it," she said. "But one day you're standing there, and they're all depending on you. You have to do it." In a mass-cal, helicopters stayed on the helipad just long enough to unload their cargo of three or four injured soldiers before they departed to make way for succeeding choppers. Litters were carried through the small admitting and discharge building and placed on stands in the ER. No one person triaged. A corpsman or nurse examined each GI to see if he had to be treated immediately. If her patient could wait, Stephanie ran to help someone else. If she yelled for help, others came. "Sometimes we'd split into two teams," she explained. "You got to know each other well and learned to trust each other's judgment."

She examined each patient fully, front and back, to find stray bullets or shrapnel. She marked the site of every injury and wrote it down for the x-ray crew. She started IVs in each arm, drew blood, and cleaned the guys. "We washed everything to death," Stephanie said. "We had four-liter bags of saline irrigation fluid to wash out abdomens. It would wash through the belly and onto the floor. We just didn't want to miss anything." All the patients were started on antibiotics. Even so, were it not for their basic good health, many more soldiers would have died of massive infection.

Most mass-cals went on for several hours. Stephanie remembers one in which injured soldiers began arriving at nine in the morning, and she did not return to her room until 2:00 AM the following day. One-hundred-forty patients went through the ER that day. Everyone was blown apart; bodies were everywhere. Limbs were bagged, tagged, and set outside the door of pre-op. She does not know where they were taken.

When injured soldiers came in as a group, each GI wanted his buddy cared for first. It was hard on the staff, particularly when they knew that the buddy could not be helped. "If you tried to break their bonds, it really destroyed them," Stephanie said. "So, you left the first soldier, went and took care of the other one, and by the time you returned to the first, he was willing to let you do something for him because his buddy had gotten attention." In the corner of the ER was a screened-off area for soldiers who were injured so badly they were expected to die. Once, when Stephanie had to put a soldier into the corner, his buddy went crazy. "Oh Lord," she said, "talking to him was so hard. They just really had a bond."

Stephanie remembers many good times at the 24th Evac— softball games, shaving cream battles on the ward, wheelchair races in the ER, and wild parties. She has never forgotten the people she worked with, or the camaraderie the staff shared with the patients. She and Joanne Kane Halcomb even beautified the 24th—a difficult task—when they planted bright yellow marigolds at the entrance to Ward 2. They imported dirt from off-post because of Long Binh's barren soil. But, like every nurse who served in Vietnam, Stephanie made it through her year one day at a time, meeting the needs of one patient at a time, stifling her emotions, and not thinking about the war that surrounded her. "There was just so much I could allow in," she said, "or it would have ruined me." She left Vietnam in June, 1971, at the age of twenty-two.

• • • •

I visited Stephanie, now Stephanie Genthon Kilpatrick, soon after my return to the States, but we talked little of Vietnam. We had put it behind us. Only in October, 1991, when I interviewed her for this book, did we discuss the war. At first she was reluctant to share her memories. Her recollections were private, filled with people who were precious to her. She worried about dredging up feelings she had long since buried for her emotional self-protection. As we visited,

Stephanie began to relax. Each story followed more closely on the one before it. Details became richer. She asked as many questions of me as I asked of her. Eventually, the tears we shed in laughter equaled those we shed in sadness. I had packed my tape recorder and was ready to leave for the airport when I found Stephanie crying quietly at her kitchen table. There was one story she had not told me, one patient she had not shared. Now that I was leaving, the time had come to let him go.

The soldier in the ICU was no more than a boy, and he was dying. He had multiple abdominal wounds. Tubes connected him to the equipment around him. One morning at about five, he asked Stephanie for a glass of orange juice. "I told him he couldn't have anything to drink," she tearfully explained. He answered, "Stephanie, I'm dead anyway. It doesn't matter." "OK," she said, "Let me see." She called the doctor, who said "no," so Stephanie gave him nothing. Fifteen minutes later he was dead.

Stephanie and I attended the July, 1993, reunion of the 24th Evacuation Hospital in Washington, DC. It included a visit to the Vietnam Veterans Memorial, "the Wall."

Being there with friends from Vietnam brought to life the guys in the blue pajamas. Just before we left the site, Stephanie purchased a cup of orange juice at a small refreshment stand near the Wall. Then she carefully carried it down the walk in front of the black granite monument until she stood before the panel inscribed with the names of the soldiers who died in 1971. She placed the orange juice at the foot of the panel, turned slowly, and quietly walked away.

•   •   •   •

When Joanne Kane Halcomb learned I was working on this book, she wrote to tell me a story about Stephanie:

...Her room was the first in hooch #3, mine was the last, so I had to walk by her room to get to mine. She often left her door open. Most of us did, probably as an open invitation so we wouldn't have to be alone. As I walked by, she was standing in front of her chest of drawers. Since she was sobbing, I went in. She was working on what looked like a

long tape of paper. Through her tears, she was scribbling the full names of every kid who had died in the last couple of days. The list was enormous. She had been doing it all along. I told her to stop. She had to let them go to survive this herself. I remember she turned to me so solemnly and said through her tears, "But someone has to. Someone has to remember their names." Years later, when the Wall was dedicated with all those thousands upon thousands of names, I got a shiver. I cried, and then I smiled. I knew we could really all begin to forget the individual pains because their names will always be remembered. They weren't numbers anymore.

• • • •

CHAPTER SEVEN

• • • • • • • •

"...they were dying so fast."

"Mary, come look at this!" called corpsman Chris Slavsky. He was standing at the bathroom door between Wards 7 and 8. It was almost midnight. The two of us had been running all evening, but finally, most of the soldiers were asleep, the IVs were on time, and even our sickest GIs were stabilized. Now I was afraid something had happened to one of our patients. I ran into the bathroom, where Chris, with a smile on his face, silently pointed to the small window high on the outside wall. There, illuminated by the bathroom's fluorescent lights, were two gecko lizards pressed against the windowpane, one astride the other. "I couldn't let you miss this," he said. "It's like watching an X-rated movie!"

• • • •

Twenty years later, I visited Chris at his home in the foothills of the Rocky Mountains, just north of Colorado Springs. I had explained to him that it was important to me to include his emergency room experiences in this book. "I don't have much to say," he protested, "but I'll tell you what I can remember." He took a day off from work and for five hours we sat at his kitchen table. Without a break, he told his story.

A Michigan native, Chris attended Adams State College in Colorado. There, he spent more time hiking, hunting, fishing, and skiing than cracking the books. "All I really wanted to do was get out into the mountains and hike," he said. He flunked out in 1968 during his junior year, lost his student draft deferment, and immediately enlisted in the Army. He remembered, "I was pretty aware I was going from a 2S [student deferment] to a 1A [eligible to be drafted] classification, and I didn't want to end up in the infantry. I just wanted to get it over with, but not be drafted. I wanted to have some control over what I'd be doing. My brother had been a medic, and I thought it would be interesting. After basic, I got as much specialized training as I could to put me in a better situation. I figured the more training I had, the more valuable I would be. I might be on my own at a battalion aid station in the field, but at least I wouldn't be with an infantry platoon in the bush." At the time Chris was weighing his options, seventy percent of American infantry soldiers were draftees.

Chris' advanced training made him a 91C— the Army's equivalent of a licensed practical nurse. He arrived in Vietnam in October, 1970, and spent a week at the 90th Replacement Battalion waiting for orders. "While I was at there," he remembered, "I stopped into the 93rd Evacuation Hospital [on Long Binh Post, across the road from the 90th] to look up nurses I had known at Letterman [General Hospital, in San Francisco—his first assignment]. One of them introduced me to the sergeant in charge of corpsmen. I told him my qualifications, and he put in a request for me. Then he assigned me to the emergency room. I felt real lucky to go to the 93rd."

The 93rd Evacuation Hospital, on the perimeter of Long Binh Post, was built a year before the 24th. Though American casualties had significantly dropped off after the Cambodian invasion of the previous May, Chris discovered the emergency room had no problem staying busy. "Three nights after I arrived," he said, "I was asleep in the barracks when the sergeant in charge of the emergency room ran in yelling, 'Casualties!' I bolted out of bed. There were ten or fifteen guys that night, shot up and in a lot of pain."

Chris learned quickly what to do when an injured GI was put in front of him. "I cut off the soldier's uniform to see where he was hit," he explained. "The most obvious wound frequently wasn't the worst. I flushed the wounds with saline fluid and got the GI ready for surgery by putting in IVs and starting blood. I'd be in either the emergency room or the pre-op unit next door, trying to keep the guys stabilized until they could go to the OR. Some soldiers came in having lost so much blood, I don't know how they survived to get to the ER. When I started IVs, the wounds would start bleeding again, but it would be the IV fluid coming out of them. How they could maintain a high enough blood pressure until we could get something into them, I don't know. We'd get some blood back in their bodies, and they'd end up living." If a soldier needed blood quickly, Chris put pumps around the bags to push it in faster. There were times when he had blood going into the GIs through four lines at the same time. "We'd get a bunch in— six, seven, eight, ten—who were bleeding so much, when we were cleaning up afterwards, we felt like we were ankle deep in blood," he said. "It was pretty severe."

In a mass-casualty situation, the doctors often could not leave the OR to treat minor fragmentation wounds caused by pieces of metal from grenades or booby traps, so Chris went to work. "I would clean them up the best I could and get some of the metal out," he recalled. "Once the fragments got into the muscle they were so hard to find. I could feel them on top lots of times, but I just couldn't get to them. If I couldn't get them out, surgeons in the States or Japan would operate with x-rays and try to reach the metal."

Soldiers who had been burned were the worst. "One night," Chris remembered, "a young guy came in so badly burned, his fatigues had been burned off. He had just his boots on. He was still awake and aware he was dying. He didn't last long, but it hurt us to watch him go through the pain. That night, all of us cried."

Chris found it difficult to deal with soldiers who arrived at the hospital already dead. "Seeing just how badly they were screwed up," he said. "When GIs came in from the field in body bags, I had to kinda sort out who they were. I tagged them, cut off their rings and got them ready to be examined by the doctor who listed the cause of death. In some cases, there wasn't much for the doctor to examine. I remember one soldier who had stepped on a mine. All that was left of him was his torso above the diaphragm. The rest was stuffed down into the end of the body bag— everything that could be scraped up."

GIs who had been pulled out of rivers were brought to the ER. "After floating a week or so in the water, they were all bloated up and unrecognizable," Chris recalled.

Some injuries illustrate how the character of the war had changed by late 1970. Large-scale military operations of earlier years had given way to days filled with aimless patrols through dense jungles. Soldiers spent most of their time trying to avoid enemy mines and ambushes, at times unsuccessfully. "One guy came in after taking a direct hit from an enemy rocket in the abdomen." explained Chris. "It went right through him. It never went off, but it just about tore the guy in two." Accidents also caused severe injuries. Chris remembered a GI who arrived after a percussion grenade accidentally went off in his hand. "I cut off what was left of the hand with a bandage scissors," he said.

Many of the cases seen in the emergency room reflected increasing demoralization among the GIs. From the time the first units of U.S. troops were withdrawn in July, 1969, soldiers sent to Vietnam knew they were politically expendable. They realized that their fates rested with men in Paris who had taken months to agree on the shape of a negotiation table. They believed that the American people had rejected them or, at best, had forgotten them. And still, they were expected to go into the jungle to shoot at people and to be shot at. "I felt real bad for the guys in the bush," said Chris. "They had a lot of fear and a lot of anger. It was very discouraging to be in Vietnam then, to see what was happening to the soldiers. You couldn't understand what we were trying to accomplish by being there. Whatever it was, we sure didn't seem to be doing it the way it needed to be done."

Heroin overdoses were common, as were suicide attempts. Some GIs tried to hang themselves; others had self-inflicted wounds. One day, a soldier was brought in after shooting himself in the leg at close range with an M-16. "The x-ray showed six or eight inches of his femur gone, shattered into about fifty pieces," Chris explained. "He didn't realize how badly he was going to damage himself when he did it. A .45 would have passed through his leg. Instead, he totally destroyed it." Soldiers arrived in groups after bar brawls. "Usually, the guys had busted each other's heads open," said Chris. "There were so many of them that I got good at sewing them up."

Vietnamese civilians came to the emergency room after auto accidents. Just west of the 93rd Evacuation Hospital was Highway One, the principal north-south artery in Vietnam. For the twenty-miles between Long Binh and Saigon, the road was a four-lane paved highway. Trucks and semi-trailers rode beside hundreds of Vietnamese people on bicycles and small Honda motorbikes, making it a dangerous stretch of road. At the exit gate of Long Binh, a sign warned everyone leaving the post: "You Are About to Enter the Most Dangerous Area in Vietnam, a Public Highway." The warning was particularly valid after a rain and especially for Vietnamese families who often rode on a single motorbike. The father drove with a child on his lap, while another child sat on the handlebars. The mother was behind the father, with a third child or grandmother behind her. It was an inexpensive way to travel because motorbikes with 50cc engines were not taxed. But rain-slicked roads could be fatal to a whole family. Chris remembers one afternoon during monsoon season when a pregnant woman was carried in with a large group of injured civilians. She died almost immediately from internal injuries. Doctors did an emergency Caesarean section in an effort to save the baby. Unfortunately, the infant had already died.

Another accident victim was a Vietnamese officer. "I ran to him as he was being wheeled into the ER," Chris said. "When I checked him, I realized the back of his skull was completely blown off. Apparently, he had been in the accident with three or four other soldiers and he probably thought he was the only one who had lived. We figured he thought it was the honorable thing to die with his friends, so he stuck a gun in his mouth and blew his brains out. The other guys had come in with him. None of them was dead."

Some civilian injuries were peculiar to a war zone. "A Vietnamese man came in with a small grenade in his thigh," he remembered. "It had been fired at close range and it hadn't gone off. We didn't know for sure what would set it off, so we carefully moved him around on the litter. On the way to the OR, another corpsman and I hit a wall as we tried to maneuver his gurney around a corner. We stopped dead in our tracks." A surgeon volunteered to operate through a small window in the middle of a sandbagged OR. An ordnance team stayed with him in the operating room and carefully placed the grenade in a special box after the doctor removed it. It never went off.

Another night, a little Vietnamese girl came in with a metal fragment imbedded in her chest from an exploding booby trap. "No one knew if she had discovered the booby trap or if she had been involved in making it when it exploded. That's just the kind of life it was," Chris said simply.

He was anxious to leave the ER after six months. "I was starting to get a little dingy," he remembered. "It was hard to see so many guys totally ripped apart, to see the damage done to the human body. I was so tired of the blood and the pain and the suffering. The guys were so young and they were dying so fast. And I worried about the people who lived when they probably should have been allowed to die."

In April, 1971, the 93rd Evac closed, and Chris gladly moved to the 24th Evac at the center of Long Binh Post. "The day before I left, a hooch 200 yards away from mine got rocketed. No one was in it, but it scared the shit out of me. We had a couple of guard positions adjacent to the hospital that we had to man because we were on the perimeter. I was nervous about it, but it wasn't all that bad. I just kept my eyes and ears open. But this was a little close."

At the 24th, Chris first worked in the Vietnamese civilian unit across the road from the hospital and then in the neurosurgical intensive care unit on Ward 5. It was a tough rotation for him. "I felt I didn't know enough to take care of those guys and I really felt bad for them. There didn't seem to be a lot of hope for them. I wonder sometimes if any of them are still alive. Some of them knew what had happened but they couldn't communicate. They could hear but not speak. One guy had taken a round in front of his temple. It went right through and out the other side. It took out his two eyes. He was conscious. He could talk, but he couldn't believe he lost his eyes. He thought when the bandages came off, he'd be OK."

After a month, Chris came to work with us in internal medicine. "Just when I started to learn how to take care of the guys on neurosurgery, I was transferred," he recalled. Because of his skills, he spent most of his time working in the medical ICU. "It was a whole new aspect of patient care," said Chris, "more like a big-city hospital,

not a wartime situation. Any idea I'd had of what war was, this wasn't
it. But it was interesting, especially taking care of the Thai patients
with blackwater fever and the guys with cerebral malaria."

Chris left Vietnam and the Army in October, 1971. During
the next eight years, I saw a lot of him. When my husband, Doug, and
I lived in Denver, we camped and skied the Rockies with Chris and
his wife, Carolyn. We spent numerous holidays together. He and I
often talked about the patients we had cared for in internal medicine.
But Chris never told me about his experiences in the emergency room,
nor had he said anything to Carolyn. Despite the protests that he had
little to say, he had forgotten nothing. For twenty years, the details
had been arranging themselves in his mind, waiting for someone to
turn on a tape recorder.

• • • •

CHAPTER EIGHT

•   •   •   •   •   •   •

"...balls to the wall."

"Lieutenant Reynolds, you have a visitor," shouted the guard at the 90th Replacement Battalion. "It's a Mr. Miller." I had been in Vietnam for eighteen hours, deprived of sleep, outfitted in fatigues and started on malaria prophylaxis. I hardly felt like the person who had boarded the plane in California two days earlier. Suddenly, with the announcement that John Miller had come to visit me, normalcy returned to my life.

John and I had met ten months earlier in a bar at Ft. Sam Houston, Texas, where I was in basic training. He was a warrant officer pilot stationed at Ft. Sam to finish a medical training course before leaving for Vietnam. John had not been worried about going to the war. Twenty-one years old with boyish, all-American good looks, he believed he was immortal. And like all pilots, he found in aviation the province of the gods. If the Army would let him fly, he would go anywhere. During his nine months in-country, he had flown medical evacuation (dustoff) helicopters, ferrying wounded soldiers from combat to hospitals. Now, in one of those air ambulances, he had literally dropped in to welcome me to the war.

•   •   •   •

John and I lost track of each other after he left Vietnam. Eighteen years later, with no warning, he phoned me on a hot, sticky, summer night. When I heard his voice, I must have looked like I was talking to a ghost. My daughters, seeing my face blanch, ran to get their dad to help me. Two years later, I visited John at his Florida home to interview him for this book. It was as much a joy to greet him there as it had been to see him at the 90th Replacement Battalion so many years before.

John grew up in Glen Ellyn, Illinois. In January, 1968, he failed out of Trinity University in San Antonio after one festive semester, and his draft classification immediately became 1A. With Uncle Sam at his heels, he stopped at an Army recruiting station to investigate his options. "I saw a rack of brochures before I talked to the Army recruiter," John remembered. "On the cover of one was a guy standing in a swamp holding a rifle over his head. Another pamphlet had a young pilot posed in front of his helicopter with a beautiful sunset behind him. That's the one I grabbed. I knew if I waited to be drafted, I'd find myself in the swamp."

In flight school, luck put John in the cockpit of the dustoff helicopter and not in a gunship. "I was waiting to use the phone one day," he said. "The guy on it, a friend of mine, was telling the selection officer in Washington he wanted to fly dustoff. There were two slots available, so he turned to me and asked if I wanted the other."

The origin of the term "dustoff" is unknown. Some pilots believe it was the radio call sign of the first medevac pilot killed in the Vietnam War. Others think the term comes from the helicopter rotor blades that "dust everybody off" on landing. One of my instructors at Ft. Sam, a dustoff pilot himself, insisted it was an acronym for "Devoted, Unswerving Service To Our Fighting Forces."

Most Army dustoff pilots were warrant officers, a rank that placed them between enlisted men and regularly commissioned officers. They had no administrative responsibilities; their sole job was to fly. "We were fast, balls to the wall, and proud of it!" John said. "We were crazy. In fact, the term 'crazy helicopter pilot' is redundant. It was like giving every senior boy in high school a '57 Chevy with a 327 engine, positraction, and dual quads under the hood. Instead, we got a million-dollar Huey to race around the skies with." All the warrant officer pilots were young, some only eighteen when they arrived in-country. "Maybe the military figured they couldn't have gotten any-one else to do our job," suggested John. "They needed youngsters who weren't yet familiar with the word 'mortality.' In fact, in military avia-tion, NAFOD refers to an individual who has 'No Apparent Fear of Death.' It's a synonym for pilots up until about age 23."

John arrived in Vietnam in February, 1970, and was assigned to the 45th Medical Company on Long Binh Post. "I felt just like a high school freshman," he remembered. "Like everyone else, I was given my own baseball cap with the unit insignia on it. When we got the cap, we had to paint the button on top red. That meant we were 'newbies' or 'peter pilots.' As soon as the helicopter you were flying took a few hits, you could take the red button off your cap, demon-strating to everybody in the unit that you had 'lost your cherry.'" Two weeks into his tour, John lost his.

In April, he was reassigned to the 159th Dustoff Detach-ment at Cu Chi, halfway between Saigon and the Cambodian border. "I was the replacement for a copilot who had been in-jured in a crash after the aircraft commander took a bullet in the head," recalled John. "Within a short time, I became an aircraft commander myself and was given the radio call sign of 'Dustoff 152.'"

The 159th was a small unit; twelve warrant officers flew six helicopters (D- and H-model Hueys). Thirty enlisted men served as medics, or crew chiefs, or in personnel. The unit supported U.S. forces, particularly the 25th Infantry Division, as well as ARVN (Army of the Republic of Vietnam) troops operating in the area. They also picked up injured civilians.

An aircraft commander, copilot, medic (corpsman), and crew chief made up each helicopter crew. The medic took care of the patients, while the crew chief was the mechanic for the Huey. Crews flew on a twenty-four-hour rotating call schedule, starting at 8:00 AM. One crew, designated "first-up," handled all missions for the day unless there was a firefight (skirmish) with heavy casualties. Then, the "second-up" and "third-up" teams were called. Normally, a pilot would be assigned first-up one day, have a couple of days off, and then be assigned to second or third-up.

Field commanders classified missions when they called for a pick-up. "The number one call was urgent," said John, "and the number one urgent was an American GI wounded in combat. It meant launch NOW! The crew would run to the aircraft and take off immediately. The control tower suspended all other flights. Soldiers who were less severely wounded got picked up on priority missions within two to four hours. Malaria cases or GIs with low-grade combat injuries were called routine. We had twenty-four hours to evacuate them from the bush."

The dispatcher who called the first-up crew told them where to pick up the patient. "He'd read off the map coordinates of the patient site or give us the general location related to a known city or landmark," explained John. "He'd let us know if the LZ [landing zone] was "cold" [no enemy action] or "hot" [fighting going on]. If the LZ was cold, I concentrated on the technicalities of the flight while my copilot stayed on the radio to request artillery units enroute to hold their fire. If the LZ was hot, things became even more complicated. Not only did we have to fly the Huey, we both never stopped talking on the freakin' radio. On the way in, one pilot would be talking to artillery while the other would be talking with the guy at the pickup site about popping a flare or smoke grenade to guide us in. We also had to contact the pilots of the gunships who were providing gun cover for us to discuss the location of the enemy and the best approach to the LZ. Often, the gunships were already in the firefight. If not, we'd meet them at a designated point to go in together."

Nights were the wildest. If the pickup was at a base camp under siege at night, John recalled it was like "landing in the middle of a giant Fourth of July fireworks display gone out of control. Everything was going off at once: the flash of the cannon, the tracer spray of automatic weapons, and the red stream of gunship fire." Artillery-launched parachute flares illuminated the whole scene. "Imagine," he said, "your body and mind absorbing all of that at once and then add the heat and sweat, the spit drying in your mouth, the pounding of the rotor blades, the constant radio chatter, and the 'whump' of grenades from the gunship clearing the path. And while all this frenzy is going on, your adrenaline is pumping, but you can't do anything about it because the Huey requires your arms and legs to operate at one-quarter speed. I have heard veterans say they haven't felt fully alive since they left Vietnam, and it's no wonder. Away from that, none of us felt alive."

Gunships provided support for evacuations because dustoff helicopters did not have guns mounted on them. Gunship and dustoff pilots had great respect for each other. "One night," John remembered, "we had to pick up a patient in jungle that was so thick it made landing impossible, and we had to drop a hoist to bring him up. The region was a little warm, enemy-wise, and Cobra gunships covered us. They were above us, and we descended with all our lights off. When we slowed to a hover just above the trees, 'BINGGG,' we put on the landing lights and lit up the whole damn place, making us a giant target. In less than a minute, we swung the wounded man into the aircraft, stowed the hoist, doused the landing lights, and got out of there. We radioed our thanks to the Cobra pilots as we headed for the hospital and they went to their home base. One of them, obviously impressed with our performance, answered, 'Hey, you guys must have brass balls to be doin' that sort of thing.' We returned the compliment."

Dustoff pilots knew they could be shot out of the sky at any time. Even if the aircraft were not fired on, each mission could end in a fiery crash. John was in one major crash soon after he started flying out of Cu Chi. "It was a routine mission," he recalled. "The helicopter landed on a small square of dirt in a rice paddy. In a flare maneuver, just before touchdown, the nose of the helicopter comes up and the tail drops slightly. That particular day without us realizing it, the tail rotor dipped into the water when we landed and damaged the gearbox assembly attached to it. On takeoff, when we reached an altitude of about 300 feet, the tail rotor began to vibrate, first a little, then a little more. After a minute or so, in one very violent vibration, the gears tore themselves apart and both the gearbox and rotor blades fell off. The tail of the aircraft went up, the nose dropped, and the helicopter flew sideways. We couldn't land that way because we would have rolled up in a burning ball, so the pilot slowed us down for a landing in a field of rice paddies. He decreased the speed to the point that we started to spin round and round like a top. Then he cut power to stop the spinning. From 150 feet in the air, we went down into a paddy. He couldn't have aimed better. Except for bumps and bruises, no one was hurt." Pilots of a second dustoff, having watched the terrifying spin and crash, came to the rescue. Within twenty-four hours of the incident, John returned to the flight schedule. "I was suddenly aware of my mortality," he said.

Just before he left the country, John had a second tail-rotor accident. "I was too cocky," he remembered. "There was a new guy with me and I was showing off, hot-rodding a bit. We flashed into a hot area and landed the wrong way. I should have turned the tail of the Huey more toward the enemy. As I touched down, we began to take fire. Soldiers on the ground virtually threw the patients on board and within seconds, we were airborne. After we had climbed to a safe altitude, we realized bullets had severed the tail rotor chain. I was flying sideways again! This time, though, the motion wasn't as pronounced, and I knew I could make a running landing. I requested an emergency landing at Bien Hoa Air Force Base because they had the longest runways in the region. Ground crews covered the runway with a two-foot layer of foam to minimize any chance of fire, and we began our descent. Suddenly, from nowhere, an Air Force rescue helicopter cut in front of us. I veered off, flew in a wide circle, and restarted my approach. At the same time, I told the Air Force pilot that while I appreciated his being there to help, I thought I'd be fine *if I had enough room to land*. The second time, he stayed out of the way. We touched down and slid to a stop. No one was hurt. While we waited for a pickup, I vaguely recall being told by a high-ranking Air Force officer that he was not too pleased his runway, built for jets, had to be closed and foamed for one little-bitty Huey, and it wasn't even an Air Force helicopter! Because he outranked us, we just thanked him for his help and quickly moved the patients into the second-up helicopter which had come to rescue us."

Fortunately, the dustoffs did not take fire often. "I think maybe the enemy lowered their weapons when they saw the red cross on the side of the helicopter," guessed John. "Possibly the word had spread throughout the Cu Chi community that we'd transport anyone who needed help. We brought in a lot of Vietnamese patients."

John loved flying the Huey, calling it "an amazing workhorse that wouldn't let you down in a tight place." Though the aircraft was

limited by weight to four crew members plus eight additional people,
John heard of times when a Huey departed under fire with eighteen
or twenty people onboard. Normally, crew members stacked three
litters crosswise in the back of the helicopter. They put a fourth on
the floor when necessary, but that did not leave much room for the
medic and crew chief to work. Four seats for ambulatory patients or
passengers were tucked behind the stacked litters.

When the patients came on board, the medic and crew chief
worked as one person. "It was overwhelming what they were asked to
do," John remembered. "They had to take care of those guys right out
of the field. They were so capable. Incredibly, the medics could start
an IV while bouncing along in the helicopter, at night, with only a
flashlight with a red lens to work by. They were so concerned and
they saw so much—GIs with body parts missing, Vietnamese kids
with shrapnel wounds, old women and men who had tripped mines,
young soldiers who would be talking and trying to sit up, but who
would die on the way to the hospital. Up front, we flew the helicopter
and talked on the radio; our helmets blocked the sounds. Unless a
patient was screaming, or the medic described the scene over the in-
tercom, we could distance ourselves from some of the horror. But in
the back, there was no escape."

No one talked about the missions. After most rescues, the
crews returned to base and tried to forget. They shifted their attention from getting through the mission to getting to the bottom of a
glass. "We cared," John remembered. "We cared a lot and we were
proud of what we did. But we were able to get away from it because,
unlike the infantry soldiers, we commuted to war. No matter how
horrible it was, we put it all behind us when we came back to base at
the end of the day. There was always a party, only the rooms changed.
There were parties and movies and barbecues and dirty movies and
horseshoes, and a lot of drinking. We drank ourselves into stupors to
the sound of Creedence Clearwater Revival."

Alcohol was an effective anesthetic, but it could not allevi-
ate all the pain. One evening, against a crimson Vietnamese sunset,
John watched ARVN soldiers prepare a cargo net for a Chinook
pickup. The Chinook was a huge helicopter called the "shit-hook,"
because it could lift anything. That night, its cargo net, which easily

could carry two cars, was being filled with the bodies of dead Vietnamese soldiers. "Watching the big bird take off with its ghastly cargo slung underneath," said John, "I felt empty, and I thought, 'What the hell for?' I must have happened onto that scene sometime toward the end of my tour when I was thinking, 'What the hell for?' about a lot of things."

By January, 1971, John was "short": he had fewer than fifty days left in-country. "Short-timers' syndrome" struck when soldiers broke one hundred days left in-country and reached fever proportions when they dropped below ten. At the 24th Evac, because of their preoccupation with going home, "single-digit midgets" were pulled from ICU duty whenever possible. In the bush, "short" infantry soldiers had no similar option for light duty, and they became overly cautious and dangerous to themselves. The same was true of dustoff pilots. "As his DEROS approached, the pilot's NAFOD [No Apparent Fear of Death] titer got dangerously low," John recalled. "We all knew too well the stories of pilots who had been killed with just a few days to go. Guys going home soon only wanted to fly peaceful third-up missions picking up malaria cases or rescuing soldiers who had severely cut themselves opening their C-rations."

John had to fly first-up missions right to the end, one of several command decisions that made him angry. "Our unit had been moved back to Long Binh when the Cu Chi base was turned over to the ARVNs," he explained. "Out at Cu Chi, we were a small, close-knit detachment operating on our own. At Long Binh, we were too close to the bigwigs' headquarters. There were too many 'higher-ups' close by, hatching too many looney ideas to interfere with the smooth operation of a combat unit. I really lost it when I heard that some high-ranking idiot was considering having the dustoff helicopters painted white because we were on a 'mission of mercy.' Nothing like making the Huey a bigger target than it already was!" (In fact, the helicopters were painted white in 1972.)

Days before he left Vietnam, John observed how far the military commanders of 1971 had distanced themselves from their troops. "I was in the dispatcher's office when a request came in for an urgent pickup," John recalled. "The soldier who took the call looked up and asked me to find the first-up crewmembers. I said, 'Why don't you ring the alarm bell like you always do?' The soldier hung his head and answered, 'Because the commander's having a uniform inspection and doesn't want to be disturbed.' It made me so damn mad, I think I rang the bell myself. After that, all I could think about was flyin' careful, receivin' my orders back to the States, and gettin' the f— out of there."

When he came home from the war, John was one of thousands of warrant officers given an early discharge by an Army reducing its ranks. He went through a series of odd jobs, then returned to college at Embry-Riddle Aeronautical University in Daytona Beach. John was a far more serious student the second time around. Within three years, he had a baccalaureate degree in aeronautical engineering and a commercial pilot's license. He yearned to fly with a commercial carrier. But with no civilian jobs available, he joined the Navy and served for six years as a flight instructor. He was married and became the father of two sons. By 1981, in the throes of a divorce, for the first time he addressed feelings he had suppressed about the war. John left the military once more in June, 1982, this time as a conscientious objector.

"A conflict started within me in Vietnam," he explained, "but I didn't know it. To survive the war, I had to resign myself to my own microcosm of fly-to-the-pickup-site- and-evacuate-innocent-people-who-have-shrapnel-wounds-or-soldiers-with-gunshot-wounds. Because I individualized the situation, I was all right. But the whole year, I was greatly affected by seeing the 'bottom line of war,' and I didn't even know it. I unconsciously wrestled with great inner turmoil for a period of ten years, incapable of expressing the feelings and dealing with them openly. When I finally faced what was in me, the conflict was pretty apparent: I was a member of the military and I was appalled by the results of military force. I was a member of the military and I was uncomfortable about my individual contribution to it. I was a member of the military and I began to think that peace efforts were hampered by the very existence of the military. My beliefs were at odds with my actions. So I left."

John resigned from the Navy ten years after Vietnam, but three experiences he'd had during the war fired his resolve to do so. The first occurred soon after U.S. forces were ordered into Cambodia in May, 1970. To support the incursion, his unit was moved to Tay Ninh, near the Vietnam-Cambodian border. The usual flight rotation schedule was abandoned. All the helicopters were in the air all the time. The invasion was two weeks old when John set a personal record of twelve straight hours in the pilot's seat. "Several times during the invasion we carried civilians whose villages had been destroyed by errant U.S. artillery," said John. "In one village, no one was killed, but nearly everyone in the village had been wounded by shrapnel. We flew entire families with shrapnel injuries to the hospital: grandparents, pregnant women, babies, and children."

The second experience took place months later when John received a call he remembers vividly. "I think I could go to Vietnam right now, get in a helicopter, and fly right to the same LZ," he said. "The call was for an 'urgent GI with wounds from a booby-trap' barely a mile southwest of the base at Cu Chi. It hadn't been a hot area for quite a while, so we were surprised. As we landed, I saw five or six men standing by a clump of trees. Two moved toward us, carrying a stretcher. The injured soldier had been attempting to defuse a Bangelor torpedo when it exploded. He lost a leg and parts of both arms. His head, trunk, and one leg were intact. What was left of the other leg was sticking straight up in the air. Only about twelve inches of his thigh remained, and as the stretcher passed by my door, I could see the purple flesh bouncing around the shattered bone. Everything else was gone. Incredibly, the soldier was awake and aware of what was happening."

The Cu Chi pickup left a permanent mark on John. Perhaps because the day was so beautiful, or because the site was so close to camp in an area that was considered safe, or because the countryside was so quiet, he had time to appreciate the waste of one human being. He followed the progress of the soldier, and during the following week, was invited several times to visit him in the hospital. "I just couldn't do it," he said softly. "I couldn't bring myself to, though now I wish I had."

A final defining event came when John was summoned in the middle of the night to transport a Vietnamese woman having birth difficulties from a village south of Cu Chi to a hospital in Saigon. "The medic was urging me to fly as fast as possible to the Vietnamese hospital," said John. "Suddenly he cried, 'Uh oh, it's comin' out, it's comin' out, what do I do?' and then a couple of minutes later he said, 'You can slow down now, the baby's been born.' " John's eyes filled with tears as he continued, "When I used to tell this story, I always finished it with a philosophical statement about 'the miracle of birth giving us hope amidst the chaos and horror of war.'" In fact, the baby had been born dead, and it took John almost ten years to admit it to himself.

"I needed to believe the baby was alive," he explained. "I needed to hang on to life because subconsciously, the human spirit in me had seen so much horror mission after mission after mission for the entire year I was in Vietnam. The caring soul within me was beaten and abused every time it witnessed the extremes to which men go in war. War is 100% destruction, thorough, complete and efficient. Any horror imaginable is perpetrated. Regardless of how bizarre the story is, how horrible, dreadful, or inhumane, it probably is true."

John said his experiences in Vietnam have become a source of strength to him. "Opening up and facing what happened has allowed me to turn the turmoil into a positive force," he explained. "I am someone who knows, because, unfortunately, I saw the horrors of war. And because I know, I am careful in my relationships with people. I am careful about conflict, and I am very careful about making sure people understand that I am a peaceful man. I've slowly and painfully developed my system of beliefs, not prompted by the tenets of an organized religion, but by having seen so clearly what happens when peace doesn't exist."

Now when he looks back, John remembers a special night in the helicopter. "I climbed up 'til I was above a layer of clouds, billowy clouds lit bright under a full moon. As we flew, no one spoke. Motion slowed. And for a moment, there was peace."

•   •   •   •

CHAPTER NINE

• • • • • • • •

"They just did what was asked of them, and they did it well."

It was impossible not to notice Lieutenant (Lt.) Terry Corneil in the Travis Air Base terminal. Like the other officers in the room, he had on a summer khaki uniform, but only Terry wore an infantry-blue shoulder cord and spit-shined jump boots. He was the most animated officer in his group. His gestures were expansive, his eyes were bright, and he never stopped smiling. In fact, Terry was happy to be going to Vietnam. He was confident he could take care of his troops, sure he would come home alive. The rest of his group seemed to feel the same. They swapped stories of airborne/ranger training, interrupting their conversation only when a woman walked by. The women smiled good-naturedly at their loud greetings and kept right on walking. I sat watching from the other side of the terminal, convinced I was looking at a group of first-class jerks.

Two days later, without his blue cord, spit-shined boots and friends, Terry was relatively subdued. We chatted at the 90th Replacement Battalion while we waited for Vietnamese tailors to sew names and insignia on our new fatigues. Except for size, Terry's uniform and mine differed in only two ways. We each had received the mandatory six olive-drab tee shirts and six pairs of regulation olive-drab woolen socks, as well as a pair of canvas-sided jungle boots. However, I did not get the olive-drab boxer shorts issued to men, and Terry did not have a "modesty panel" in his fatigue shirt. Reserved for women, the "modesty panel" was a piece of material that fastened from collar to waist under the shirt, effectively blocking the view of anyone curious about what lay beneath it. It was bulky, hot and uncomfortable, and within days, like so many women before me, I cut the damn thing out of the uniform with bandage shears.

Terry visited me at the 24th Evac two months after we arrived in-country. When I opened my door in response to his knock, there stood before me a man who bore so little resemblance to the cocky officer in the infantry-blue cord and the spit-shined boots, I had trouble recognizing him. He still had a ready smile, but his bravado was gone. He had lost fifteen pounds and his eyes had aged. He was no longer the lieutenant who had come to Vietnam convinced he could manage anything, certain he would "save the world from communism."

• • • •

In October, 1991, I visited Terry and his wife, Mary Neal, at their home in Virginia. He was anxious to tell his stories, to talk about his "guys," and to explain what had led to his metamorphosis.

Terry Corneil was born to be in the Army. The son of a career officer, he thrived in the military communities of his youth, because moving around and meeting new people reinforced his natural gregariousness. Though Terry spent his high school years in four different schools, he was elected senior class president for the class of '65 at Enterprise High School in Enterprise, Alabama. It seemed inevitable that one day he would follow his father's career path. He insists, however, that when he enrolled in the University of Alabama, he planned to be an orthodontist. Then Terry found Army ROTC.

ROTC at Alabama had a select unit for those who wanted a hard-core infantry experience. Terry joined the unit, and in his words, "mainlined it, and forgot all about dentistry." In June, 1969, he was the distinguished military graduate of his class. Then came airborne school, described by pilots as the place "where crazy men learn to jump out of perfectly good airplanes." Ranger school was next. The intense course covered hand-to-hand combat, running, obstacle

courses, mountain climbing, rappelling, and swamp exercises designed to prepare him for the jungle.

In Vietnam, Terry was assigned to the 2nd Battalion (airmobile) of the 5th Cavalry Regiment of the 1st Cavalry Division (2/5
Cav). The 1st Cav, with a long and illustrious history of service, was
the first American division to fight in all four regions, or Corps, of
South Vietnam. "Airmobile capability made the Cav unique," explained
Terry. "Wherever enemy activity was suspected, 1st Cav helicopters
inserted troops into the jungle and resupplied them every three days.
In other infantry divisions, soldiers carried seven or eight days' worth
of supplies, which hampered their maneuverability in the mountains
and jungles. Cav field commanders told the base camp how much
water and ammunition we needed, and where and when we wanted
to be resupplied. Because of our airmobile capability, battle was no
longer fought in a line. We could be a hundred miles deep and fight a
battle, we could be in-between, or we could fight in the rear. We had
mobility, agility, and aggressiveness. They always had to be prepared
for us."

Terry spent several weeks as an Executive Officer (XO) in
division headquarters at the Bien Hoa Army Base before he gladly
took over a field platoon at Firebase Mace. An hour's helicopter ride
northwest of Saigon, Mace was an isolated, semi-permanent base built
on land that American firepower had wrested from the jungle. It was
the operations center for the 2nd Battalion and provided artillery
support for units in the bush. Like all battalions, the 2nd was made
up of four companies: three infantry line companies and a headquarters company. Each line company had three platoons. Two rotated in
the bush at one time while the third stayed at Mace to provide security. Company commanders were captains; platoon leaders like Terry
were lieutenants.

Terry's platoon was a diverse collection of thirty-five men,
most of whom were part of the first post-lottery draft. "I had a good
platoon, a real good platoon," he said. "There was a part-Asian pineapple picker from Hawaii. We called him 'Pineapple.' He had a pock-
marked face, always wore a black headband. He would have been in
jail if he hadn't been in Vietnam. My machine gunner had been a
concert pianist with a philharmonic orchestra. One of the squad lead-

ers was a guy with a master's degree in education. A bunch of guys were high school drop-outs. We had a red-haired, blue-eyed Irish kid, 'Red,' from Chicago, and some good ol' boys from my neck of the woods. Our medic was a real good guy. We called him 'Hawkeye,' because of *M*A*S*H*. We worked well together. None of us asked if the war was right or wrong. That really wasn't up to us. We had a job to do and we did it together."

The GIs carried seventy-pound rucksacks into the bush. They were filled with food, clothes, ammo, and a life-sustaining six liters of water. Ponchos thrown on the ground served as bedding for the soldiers, while mosquito nets were their only covers. Firebase Mace resupplied them every three days, not only with water and ammo, but with critical morale-raising letters and packages from home. Chocolate-chip cookies became the most tangible connection to a past life.

The platoon had a lot of patience with their new lieutenant the first time they went into the bush to investigate VC activity. Fresh out of Ranger school, Terry wanted to impress his troops with the importance of being quiet. "I knew the VC and NVA were experts in camouflage," he explained. "The only way my unit could get the upper hand was if we saw the enemy before we were seen. Right after we arrived at the landing zone [LZ], I directed the platoon to form a circle. Then I cupped my ear with my hand to show the men I wanted them to listen, to pay attention to the jungle. Unless they knew routine sounds made by the birds, lizards, monkeys and falling leaves, I knew they wouldn't recognize any change." The platoon circled, Terry cupped his ear, and his guys looked at him as if he had lost his mind. They could not understand what he was doing, and wondered what kind of lieutenant had been sent to lead them. Seeing the puzzled expressions on their faces, Terry abandoned his gestures. "From then on," he remembered, "I gave directions *before* we boarded the helicopters."

Insertion into the jungle via helicopters was always exciting for Terry and his men. "If you want to get a 'hard on,' " he said, "you ought to go on an airmobile operation. Gunships are on your left and right side as you're coming in on the Huey. Your legs are hanging out, you're going ninety miles an hour. You see the artillery coming into the LZ to prep it. The artillery fire lifts. The gunships start firing rockets into the area just in case there's an ambush there. Then the Huey comes in at tree-top level, flares off and lands. The helicopter's not ten seconds on the LZ and guys are jumping off. It was fantastic every time, every time. I never lost the feeling. It wasn't because of any macho thing, you know...war, kill, burn, rape. That was never my mindset. I had a mission. Right or wrong, moral or immoral, I was gonna try to do a good job."

Two months after he took over the platoon, a devastating blow threatened the cohesion of the unit as well as Terry's self-confidence. His platoon was one of two inserted into the jungle at the same LZ. "The area we swept was fairly benign," he said. "Three days out, I located an appropriate site for resupply and radioed its coordinates to my company commander [CO], who was with the other platoon. It was jungle, but I was on a ridge overlooking the spot I had picked out. I told the CO that my men had set out an automatic ambush [alpha-alpha] to protect the LZ. I gave the CO its coordinates, and then asked if I should dismantle it. 'Negative,' he said. 'I've got 'em [the coordinates].'"

An automatic ambush was made up of several claymore mines linked together by blasting caps and connected to a small volt battery. A plastic spoon, placed between the battery's metal connectors, was tied to a trip wire. If someone hit the wire, the spoon pulled out, the metal connectors made contact, the electrical charge went to the blasting caps, and the claymores exploded, releasing a vicious storm of steel pellets. "The alpha-alpha provided security for the incoming resupply helicopter," explained Terry. "I had picked a well-traveled trail for ours, assuming the enemy would use the easiest approach to the landing zone and hit the mines before arriving at the LZ."

Unfortunately, the CO neglected to give the other platoon leader the ambush coordinates. "When the platoon leader hit the area," remembered Terry, "he rightfully sent a squad to cover the LZ, walk around it, and make sure there were no VC in the area. My mission was to find the LZ, theirs was to clear it. The squad he sent out walked down the trail with the automatic ambush and hit it. I was on the ridge about 500 meters away, within hearing distance. When I heard the claymores go off, I immediately got on the horn and said, 'I've got contact [with the enemy].' The CO said, 'Right, stud.' I knew I was being blamed for something but didn't know what. I said, 'I'm sorry???...' Then I heard Americans shouting." He and his men raced to help. Three GIs lay dead and several were injured severely, including the squad leader whose legs were blown off. It was a traumatic experience for Terry. Not only did he recognize that the tragic accident could have been avoided, but he saw for the first time how quickly death strikes. He said, "To see the guys you work with in a common mission, for common goals, get their lives snuffed out in a heartbeat, just that fast. It was hard."

The battalion commander flew out for an investigation and Terry and the company commander were relieved of duty in the field pending its results. "My guys knew what went on," Terry said. "Since word traveled, guys from the other platoon knew what happened. They were gonna frag [kill with a fragmentation grenade] the CO. All of a sudden, he was evac'd out of Vietnam because of an injury he had gotten three months before." He was replaced by a well-respected former sergeant, ex-Special Forces, a man Terry said he would have "followed to hell."

Not long after this disaster, a second encounter with friendly fire nearly resulted in the demise of the entire platoon. "We went in at a cold LZ," Terry remembered. "But our sergeant had just come to us from up north. He sensed we were being followed on our patrol, so we got a lot more cautious. We saw no sign of the enemy, and we were well into the mission when we found a stream. The guys hadn't showered for two weeks and since we hadn't seen any enemy activity, I gave them permission to swim. They were all anxious for fresh meat because they had been eating C-rations, and the fools stood in the water and threw grenades at the fish. It took a lot of effort, but finally I shut them up and we continued the patrol." Resupply was to take place where the platoon had landed. They arrived in the vicinity of the LZ at about 1800 (6:00 PM) their third day out. The point man approached the landing zone so quietly, he surprised six or seven NVA soldiers looking for food. Terry initiated contact and called in gunships. The NVA (North Vietnam Army) fled into the jungle, but the GIs were nervous about the approaching night. They began to relax once they put out an automatic ambush. "Then Pineapple asked to hang his hammock between two trees," Terry said. "I told him, 'Pine-apple, we ain't gonna do any hammocks. You're gonna sleep on the dad-gummed ground. It's been a spooky mission from the start and we just had contact.' Pineapple whined, 'Oh man...,' but he listened. At 2100 [9:00 PM], I radioed Firebase Mace for night defensive fires. Using coded coordinates which had been given to me by the company commander at the beginning of our mission, I asked for an artillery round to hit 1000 meters outside of our position, and then I requested a white phosphorus [Willy Pete] shell to explode 400 meters above the ground to confirm the coordinates of our location. If we needed help during the night, I wanted Mace to be right on the money with it." The soldiers heard the "boom" from Mace, followed by a whoosh. The phosphorus shell landed right where Pineapple had planned to put his hammock. Terry madly radioed, "check fire, check fire!" He said, "The shell never went off, but the entire platoon stayed awake all night, not knowing if it was a dud or was erratic, and could go off at any time. We had already surrounded ourselves with claymores for protection against the enemy. We couldn't just pick up and leave. The next morning, we broke camp without incident and met the resupply helicopters." Ordnance could not explain why the shell had not exploded, prompting the unit to ask the chaplain to say a prayer of thanksgiving. Smiling as he remembered Pineapple, Terry said the event was fairly typical of his life, "...always on the edge. Normally, he never wanted to wear a helmet. Then, during mortar attacks, he'd grab mine."

On another mission, a point man and a scout team (team leader and a shepherd dog) led the platoon. When the dog suddenly went on alert, his handler realized they were on a ridge line above an enemy bunker. "We attacked the bunker with all the firepower we had," Terry recalled. "It lasted about five or ten minutes. When it was over, I heard someone screaming behind me. It was Red, the kid from Chicago. He was yelling that he had been hit in the groin. It was real strange because I was between him and the bunker and I wasn't aware of any fire behind me. Hawkeye took a look at him and found out that he had not been hit, but that he had a leech on his penis. When my radio telephone operator [RTO] called in dustoff, the pilots wanted to know why they were needed. The RTO said, 'He has a 'Lima on his

Delta' [military code for "L on D"]. The pilots said, 'Repeat.' The RTO said, 'A Lima on his Delta.' They said 'Repeat,' again. By this time, the helicopter's approaching. Finally, the RTO shouts, 'A leech on his dick!!' We could see the 'bird' [helicopter] visibly shift on approach as the pilot started to laugh."

After eight months in-country, Terry was moved to the rear, where he was responsible for logistics and resupply. To no one's surprise, the assignment did not please him. Within weeks, however, he was able to maneuver his way back to the bush when the company commander of his old unit rotated out of Vietnam. Terry, now a captain with only three months left in-country, volunteered to replace him. As company commander, he had a tragic and personally traumatic final contact with the NVA.

"We had a basecamp on one side of a mountain," he remembered. "Intelligence told us the 33rd NVA battalion might be on the other side of the mountain. The 33rd was the same regiment whose butt the Cav had kicked several years before in I Corps (The northernmost region of South Vietnam; Long Binh was in III Corps). My company was told to find out if they were there. I had a platoon leader, a lieutenant from Arkansas, who had seven days left in-country. When the helicopter arrived with supplies for the mission, a good friend of his was the pilot, and he said to me, 'Hey, Dai-uy [Vietnamese for captain], I have so few days left, why don't I just go home on this log bird [resupply helicopter]?' I said, 'Listen, we may be going into something. I really need you. Would you mind just doing the mission for another three days and then I'll let you go?' 'Sure, no problem,' he said. He was the best, so I put his platoon in the lead. I knew it was potentially kinda sticky. The log bird had reported that on its approach they'd seen someone running through a rubber plantation back into the woodline on the other side of us."

The patrol was working its way through the plantation when the lieutenant radioed that he had discovered a hot trail at the woodline. He said he would check it out. "Not five or ten seconds after his call," Terry remembered, "all hell broke loose. I called the platoon's RTO to find out what was happening. I shouted, 'Put the LT on the line!' The RTO said, 'He can't.' I repeated, 'Put the LT on the line!' Again he said, 'He can't.' I asked what was going on, and the

RTO answered, 'The LT's dead.' I immediately grabbed my RTO and said, 'Let's go, shit's happenin' all over the place!' We went up there. He had taken it right between the eyes; he was the only one dead. I can't remember his name. I try so hard, but I can't. All I remember is Joe." After the company secured the area, four GIs wrapped Joe in a poncho and carried him out. "They left their rucksacks there, cameras in them, personal letters, " he remembered, his eyes filling with tears. "They only cared about him."

Dustoff came for Joe's body. "It was real interesting," Terry recalled. "I thought I had some hard-core guys, and I did. But there were some guys, because of the contact and how many days they had left in-country, suddenly had injuries. You know, sprained ankles. I let them out. I figured if they didn't want to be part of the company, I didn't want them." Terry called in artillery on the NVA positions. "We brought damnation on them...air force, artillery. We went back in the next day by a different route and saw a lot of blood on the trees. We didn't find any bodies. The NVA took their guys, just like we took ours. The bunkers were destroyed. We headed off what most probably would have been an attack on our base camp. For the sacrifice of one life, we were able to save so many others. The NVA was absolutely decimated. It was real difficult for me to lose Joe. He'd had three or four days left in-country when he died. It was my decision to send him in. He was the best, he ended up paying the piper."

The unit held a service for Joe at Firebase Mace. The entire company lined up, M-16 rifles with fixed bayonets positioned in the ground in front of them. A helmet sat on the top of each rifle butt. Terry cried quietly as he listened to Joe's eulogy. When it was over, the battalion commander approached him and said, "You really shouldn't cry. It's not a mark of good leadership." "I care," answered Terry. "Mark me down on my efficiency report because I cared."

Caring for each other held the GIs together. By 1971, large-scale search-and-destroy missions had been abandoned. Life for the infantry soldiers increasingly resembled the guerrilla existence of their foes. Living out of rucks, humping endless patrols through dense jungles, warding off scores of parasites, and avoiding enemy ambushes became the mind-numbing pattern of their lives. The pattern was interrupted only by senseless accidents, moments of fear, and sudden death. Battle strategy was non-existent and ideals were gone, but they were expected to fight a war. The grunts knew theirs was a holding operation, that they faced an enemy while someone in an office watched a clock. They recognized that global considerations were more important than their lives to their own government. Alone, they carried the burden of the war they fought. "Those seventeen, eighteen, and nineteen-year-olds were just doing their jobs," Terry said simply. "They weren't arrogant or brash or superior. They just did what was asked of them, and they did it well. They gave everything they had, and nobody understood or appreciated it."

The grunts felt that they were misunderstood and unappreciated not only by decision makers in Washington and Saigon, but by U.S. support forces in Vietnam, a group that outnumbered them by a ten-to-one margin. They derisively referred to soldiers on the large bases as "REMFs" (Rear Echelon Mother-Fuckers), and believed the REMFs knew nothing of what it meant to be in the bush. One evening, this animosity erupted in an encounter Terry had with a REMF colonel in a Bien Hoa officers' club. He and his lieutenants had come in from the firebase—an opportunity enlisted men rarely had. The three young officers, convinced they were the "meanest mothers in the valley," wore their jungle fatigues to the club. It was filled with "guys who drew combat pay even though they had air-conditioned hooches and running toilets," said Terry. "A couple of times when we came in, we took over the center table in front of the band. This one night, a buxom blond came out to sing, and an Air Force guy in a pure white flight suit jumped up on the stage to dance with her. It really tore us up. Someone had brought in a skull. I don't know where it came from or how it got onto our table, but we poured beer into it and started drinking out of it. A colonel at the club had his wife with him. He came over to the table and said, 'I don't think that's appropriate. My wife's offended.' I said to him, 'You're right, it's not appropriate. But *war* offends me. Now get out of here.' He said, 'Captain, I'm a colonel.' I stood up and said, 'Yes sir, I know that, but I've been in the bush. Have you?' He said, 'No.' 'Then get out of here,' I said, and he did. It was a whole different mentality. We knew the harsh realities of war. For people in the rear, war was a job and a paycheck."

Whenever he got to Bien Hoa, if he had time, Terry hitched a ride to Long Binh to visit me for what he called a "sanity check." I never knew when he was coming. Sometimes he would bring Hawkeye or some of the other guys from his unit, other times he would come alone. If I was not working, we would talk in the club at the 24th or over dinner at the USARV officers' club. During the year, I watched his bright-eyed idealism disappear in the face of the war's reality. The change was visible, particularly after the automatic ambush accident that occurred early in his tour. Slumped in a chair at the club, he repeatedly reviewed the details of the tragic event, trying to figure out what he could have done to prevent it. He no longer trusted anyone in command and, more significantly, he questioned whether he should be given a command himself.

I last saw Terry in Vietnam at the 90th Replacement Battalion officers' club, exactly a year after our arrival. He was waiting for his flight home with two of the officers I recognized from our trip over. On the way out of Vietnam, they were even louder than they had been the year before at Travis. Thankfully, they boarded the plane before mine.

As he told me his stories in 1971, his emotions mirrored what he had felt in Vietnam: pride in his troops, anger at the lack of appreciation for them in Vietnam and in the States, sadness in dealing with Joe's death, and frustration that he could remember nothing more than Joe's first name. His eyes often filled with tears. He punctuated his sentences with long pauses as he recalled a year that had meant so much to him. He said, "It was the most precious year of my life. Commanding in combat is the greatest thing that's ever happened to me. I say that not from the standpoint of killing, there's no joy in killing. My sense of satisfaction comes from having been able to take care of my troops, to take care of my soldiers' lives. It was the ultimate challenge. There is no other job that even comes close. I learned so much about myself, my strengths and weaknesses. I learned how precious life is and how frail it is. It can be gone in a second. If I could change one thing in my life, it would be to bring Joe back. But there's no way I would trade that year, that experience, for anything."

• • • •

CHAPTER TEN

• • • • • • • •

"It's not much of a war, but it's the only war we've got."

An August, 1966, CIA report speculated that the will of the North Vietnamese to win was greater than the ability of the United States to persist in Vietnam. The North would be victorious, it argued, despite a bombing campaign and the mobilization of American ground forces in the South. After reviewing the report, President Lyndon Johnson reportedly said to Defense Secretary Robert McNamara, "Hell, don't show this to anyone. Put the clamps on it. If this gets out, it will destroy the morale and spirit of our armed forces."[2] The CIA analysis was strikingly accurate, as was LBJ's prediction. In 1971, despite massive campaigns that dropped the equivalent of 700 pounds of American bombs on every man, woman and child in Vietnam and a mobilization effort that sent close to three million GIs to Southeast Asia, Americans were leaving Vietnam without a victory, and the morale of the armed forces was disintegrating.

The American soldier who arrived in Vietnam in 1965 and 1966 had a mission: to defeat the communist foe. To his mind, stopping communism in a far-off land was preferable to fighting on the coast of California. He was one with his superiors and his fellows in this mission. To the soldier of '71, nothing was clear. He was part of a withdrawing Army, yet he was being asked to fight a war. He had been in elementary school when the first American troops arrived in 1965, yet he found himself shedding blood for the same land on which they fought. The people he had come to help resented him. Friend and foe were indistinguishable. Democracy bore no likeness to the corrupt Saigon regime for which he was being asked to risk his life. Vietnamese peasants were more interested in obtaining food than in an abstract ideal of democracy. The soldier of '71 saw no purpose to his being in Vietnam.

The war's objective had changed. At first, the goal shifted from resisting communist expansion from the North to strengthening the pro-American Saigon government. In its final years under Richard Nixon, the rationale for continued involvement was geopolitical. On the world stage, the U.S. had to appear invincible. American troops had to leave the country slowly because a quick exit would expose the weakness of the South Vietnamese government and lead to an immediate communist victory. "Peace with Honor" became the driving motto. But the soldier who went to Vietnam while the U.S. was disengaging did not have the luxury of contemplating geopolitical considerations. His life was on the line. He knew only that he did not want to be the last American killed in Vietnam.

The military had changed. Focus went from analyzing battle tactics to inspecting starched fatigues. Commanders stopped developing strategic plans. In 1969, Secretary of State Henry Kissinger expressed frustration at the inability of senior officers to offer any "imaginative ideas to a new president eager for them."[3] Nor were the generals able to extricate themselves from a political effort in which they saw no clear military objectives. A 1974 survey by Brigadier General Douglas Kinnard revealed that "almost 70% of the Army generals who managed the war were uncertain of its objectives."[4] Yet, as they put almost three million Americans on the ground in Vietnam, only once did the most senior officers contemplate sacrificing their careers for their beliefs. In August, 1967—about the time Defense Secretary Robert McNamara was planning to bail out of the war— the Joint Chiefs of Staff secretly agreed to resign en masse to protest the lack of a clear policy in Vietnam. They reversed their decision the next day, believing that such an action would embarrass the president and be seen as mutiny.[5] They continued to participate in the war effort despite their opposition to its management, lending credibility to the justification we so often heard in-country: "It's not much of a war, but it's the only war we've got." Military leaders wasted their troops, they broke the trust that traditionally exists between officers and their men, and they fueled the disintegration of military morale from the top down.

The country at home had changed. Americans, tired of war, had seen too many body bags and had heard more than enough stories of drug abuse, black marketeering, and senseless slaughters. After watching U.S. soldiers put on trial for war crimes, they no longer knew if a returning soldier was a hero or a criminal. They became indifferent. Even anti-war activists turned their attention to domestic matters. Troops were coming home and fewer soldiers were being drafted. Most Americans believed all that remained to end the country's dark night was the signing of peace accords. No one cared that planeloads of fresh GIs were arriving daily in Vietnam.

The soldier himself had changed. Elimination of educational deferments and the adoption of the draft lottery diversified the forces in Vietnam. A greater proportion of older, well-educated soldiers served next to young high school dropouts. The drafted soldier of '71 had nothing in common with the career officers and NCOs he disparagingly called "lifers." He had been in the States for the anti-war protests and moratoriums and might have participated in them. He had seen thousands of his contemporaries, even friends, flee to Canada to avoid his fate. Aware of the *Pentagon Papers,* the government documents that revealed the duplicity of US involvement in Vietnam, he did not delude himself into thinking that he was part of something noble. The soldier of '71 even looked different. Love beads hung from his neck and dangled from his "boonie" (uniform jungle) hat. Peace symbols adorned his helmet and fatigues. He wanted no part of the war, but he was in the jungle.

•　•　•　•

Lieutenant Colonel (LtC.) Frank Chamberlin arrived in Vietnam in July, 1970. He was a career medical officer who had seen fourteen years of military service before orders for Vietnam provided an escape from Ft. Polk, Louisiana. "They were willing to let me stay there for another year," he said, "but I knew I'd have to go to Vietnam eventually, and I couldn't imagine conditions in a war zone being any worse than at Ft. Polk."

In February, 1971, I met Frank, one of the few board-certified cardiologists in-country, when he was called to see a young cardiac patient at the 24th Evac. He examined our patient and consulted with the ward physicians. When he finished, he took a chair, placed it next to the bed of another young patient, and sat down for a quiet chat. He repeated this procedure four times, moving his chair with him each time. Frank asked the startled GIs how things were going. Then he listened closely to their answers. His questions were patient and non-judgmental, his tone gentle. Once the soldiers saw that his concern was genuine, they relaxed. They were surprised a lifer as "old" as he (graying hair, in his early '40s) cared enough to ask and even more, to listen.

Frank welcomed every opportunity to talk with the GIs because he knew too well the burden they carried. During the first half of his tour, he had been the commander of the 17th Field Hospital, a ninety-bed facility in the central highlands at An Khe. There he shared the anger of his staff at a war that would not end and a system that kept it going. As they watched explosions across the valley, the nurses and doctors knew they would soon be hearing the sound of helicopters bringing them ravaged young men who should have been back in the States. "It seemed totally screwed up," he remembered. "We were losing people yet we stayed there. The troops weren't accomplishing anything. They were getting maimed, we were taking care of them, but nothing was happening to change the situation. My staff often asked me 'Why are we here?' and I would answer, 'We're here because we're medical people and the GIs need our help, but don't ask me why they're here, because I don't know.' "

During mass-cals at An Khe, Frank, who had done a single year of surgical internship, was pressed into OR service. "But most often," he said, "I worked with dead bodies and parts of bodies, sorting through them and determining the cause of death. I was the least valuable of any of the doctors when we were working, so I took that job myself. Besides, I didn't want to give it to one of the younger doctors. I figured I'd be better able to handle it than they could. It was the worst thing I had to do the whole year. I still have bad memories of it."

Remembering the war's carnage reawakened his frustration twenty years after he left Vietnam. Of no one in particular he demanded, "What the hell were we doing? We didn't want to be there. The Vietnamese people didn't want us there. The people back home didn't want us there. Someone wanted us there. Perhaps it just got going and kept perpetuating itself. I'd like to believe that there weren't sinister motives, like selling arms and equipment. But it sure seemed to take a hell of a long time for the government to finally say, 'This is crazy.'"

He felt the worst for the young draftees. "We [the medical staff] could at least help people," he said. "All they could do was go out in the jungle to look for Vietnamese to shoot at, and to be shot at. These young fellows became bored, afraid, disgruntled. In many cases there was bad leadership. The troops didn't like the military and they didn't want to be in Vietnam. They had the same feeling I did: what in hell are we here for?"

Frank felt several military policies invited exploitation or undermined the safety of the young GIs. He aimed his harshest words at "ticket-punching," a policy designed to give officers opportunity for career advancement. To get promoted, line officers (infantry and artillery) had to have a minimum amount of combat command time "punched" on their records. Lieutenants and captains had to put in three months, majors and lieutenant colonels needed four, colonels did six months. Rarely did a commander in Vietnam go beyond the required time; his replacement checked-in as the three, four, or six months expired. Even generals rotated commands. Although they were assigned to Vietnam for eighteen months, they rarely held a command for longer than a year because so many other generals needed combat command time to get another star.

"Ticket-punching," Frank explained, "meant that an infantry soldier who served with the same unit for a year could have three battalion commanders, four company commanders, and four platoon leaders during that year. There was no continuity. Even the best officers found they did not have time to accomplish much in the few months they were in command." Grunts, like the soldiers in Terry Corncil's platoon, had little respect for the revolving-door commanders. "But the system stayed the same throughout the war," said Frank, angrily. "No one seemed to care enough to be honest about what was happening. They only cared about promotions."

Promotions were also influenced by military awards and medals, many of which were not deserved, according to Frank. He had a personal connection to one wrongfully-awarded medal, an incident that left him seething. "In late 1970, just before the South Vietnamese Army took over the U.S. base at An Khe, it went on 'red alert,' which meant the enemy was at the post perimeter," he remembered. "An administrative officer on my staff inspected hospital guard positions to make sure sentries had adequate guns and ammo. During his rounds, he turned his ankle and reported to sick call. He did not notify me, the hospital commander. When I left the staff for another assignment, the officer nominated himself for a Purple Heart medal (given to someone who receives a war injury) and received it. It was a mockery of the severely injured patients on whom I had pinned Purple Hearts."

Abuse of the awards system not only affected the promotions of officers, but also benefited enlisted men. Frank knew of several infantry units that gave out Army Commendation Medals and Bronze Stars every time their soldiers met the minimum amount of time between awards, not because of individual valor. "In this way," Frank explained, "each soldier could receive four medals in a year's tour of duty. Because medical commands gave out far fewer medals and took longer to award them, senior NCOs on our hospital staff fell behind on the military promotion list. It was an unfair system, but I was powerless to correct it."

Another exploitation of the system involved arrival and departure dates from Vietnam. "Young GIs had little choice but to follow division orders," said Frank. "They were part of a herd. But officers and NCOs with contacts in administrative offices could arrange to arrive in Vietnam at the end of one calendar month and depart a year later during the first days of the following month. This way, they would reap an extra month's hostile duty pay and separation benefits. An Air Force policy invited similar abuse. Cargo pilots based in Okinawa loaded their planes the last day of a month, flew through Vietnam airspace to Hong Kong, and flew back the first day of the next month. Everyone who went on the flight, including passengers, collected two months of extra benefits. People were beating the system on a lot of levels. It was all acceptable to them because it was war and everyone was doing it. No one seemed to be taking the war seriously except the poor kid who had to go out on missions. Everyone else was self-serving."

Administrative changes that came with the downsizing and withdrawal of the American forces seemed like useless paper-shuffling to Frank. He described an experience that occurred several months after his arrival at An Khe. "The 8th Field Hospital at Nha Trang physically closed down," he recalled. "Since it had been the first hospital in Vietnam, the Army command wanted to keep it in-country. I was ordered to go to Nha Trang and bring the colors of the 8th Field back to An Khe. We became the 8th Field. The same people worked in the same building, but the hospital flew the 8th Field flag. I was disgusted. Hell, none of us had been there when the 8th Field came in, we didn't care about it. Any chance for unit identification was further ruined soon after when I was ordered to move my hospital to an abandoned Air Force base at Tuy Hoa."

Frank's experience was typical of changes which took place in-country as units and individuals left the country in a confusing American diplomatic and military struggle to "Vietnamize" the war—replace U.S. soldiers with ARVN troops. During his year's tour of duty, he held six administrative titles for doing three jobs.

The move of his newly-named 8th Field Hospital to Tuy Hoa further showed how official decisions could place Americans in jeopardy. "It was carried out in two steps *after* the entire 4th Infantry Division had pulled out of An Khe, leaving no infantry troops to guard the hospital in the insecure region," remembered Frank. "When the first half of the hospital departed for Tuy Hoa, two of my surgeons volunteered to wait alone in an arsenal they built to protect themselves until the second half could be moved. Nothing happened to them, but I was furious they were placed in an unnecessarily dangerous position."

Vietnamization (the effort to turn the war over to the South Vietnamese Army) backfired on the GIs still in-country. Frank said that when he first arrived in Vietnam in July, 1970, he felt safe traveling in the region just north of Saigon. By January, 1971, with

Vietnamization in full swing, he no longer felt this way. Where there once had been nine divisions of American troops, only two brigades of the 1st Cav remained to back up the inadequate ARVN forces.[6] The unsafe conditions mirrored the earliest years of the war, and reinforced for American troops how useless the conflict and loss of lives had been.

About the time Frank moved the 8th Field to Tuy Hoa, General Michael Davison asked him to join the staff of II Field Force, the largest combat command in Vietnam.

The general gave Frank a mandate to address the increasingly serious problem of drug abuse among his troops. At II Field Force, Frank quickly became disheartened not only by his work with drug-addicted GIs but by the staff officers with whom he worked. "I had a particular disdain for those who arrived in-country, lived in trailers for a year, and left without ever getting close to a combat person or a combat unit. They were hot shots on a three-star general's staff," he remarked. "They had no more idea of what went on outside the compound than they could fly."

He bitterly described what it was like to attend a staff briefing. "At a typical briefing, the general might be informed of the capture of thirty-five mess kits, seventeen radios, two rifles...all trivial stuff. I thought at the three-star level they'd be talking about personnel and munitions. Once in a while there would be activity. The general would be given statistics on casualties and captures. Casualties were down, which was good, but the military had to report some justification for going out. So they came up with numbers of enemy casualties. When you look at what they reported, I think we killed every enemy soldier five times in reports. Hell, the NVA and VC were there when I arrived and the war had been going on for five years. They were there when I left. We weren't achieving anything. It blew my mind that the general was told about captured mess kits. I guess if you didn't count the mess kits you had captured, what had you done? Who knows, maybe we significantly changed the war by the number of mess kits we captured. The general just sat there and listened to the reports. He was a career military man, a particularly good and sensitive man. It must have killed him to hear them."

Frank was appalled by what he witnessed at the higher levels of the military. But there were few GIs in Vietnam who weren't similarly disgusted. The desertion and AWOL rates showed it. Before 1968, desertions (absent without leave for more than thirty days) were fewer than those of World War II and the Korean War. By 1971, the rate had increased fourfold. Thousands of GIs routinely were absent without leave—sixty-five thousand in 1970.[7] In Saigon, a subculture of AWOL American soldiers lived with Vietnamese families for extended periods and supported themselves on the black market while they contemplated defecting to Sweden through an active pipeline. Military demoralization was rooted in Vietnam, but it extended well beyond its borders. In 1971, 250,000 men—the equivalent of ten divisions—were AWOL from Army bases throughout the world.[8]

The Army of '71 was at war with itself. Soldiers turned on superiors they saw as uncaring or threatening to their survival. Prior to 1969, the term, "fragging" (the use of a fragmentation grenade to kill a disliked officer) was not even used in Vietnam, and no statistics existed. In 1969, two hundred officers were "fragged." A year later, the figure had risen to three hundred sixty-three. In some units, troops paid bounties of hundreds or thousands of dollars to the soldier who either fragged the officer or shot him on patrol. After the battle of "Hamburger Hill" in May, 1969—the bloody ten-day effort to take a mountain only to abandon it the day after it was taken— GIs in the 101st Airborne Division reportedly offered a $10,000 bounty for the murder of the officer who ordered the attack.[9] A unit might warn the hated officer or NCO with a gas or smoke grenade to change his attitude or behavior before his men fragged him. Some officers even conducted retaliatory counterfraggings.[10] Fragging was so common that the term became part of the everyday language of U.S. soldiers in Vietnam— in the jungle, on bases, and even in the hospitals. On the wards at the 24th Evac it was not unusual to hear something like, "The major won't get off my back. I wish someone would frag her."

From the Mekong Delta in the south to the demilitarized zone (DMZ) up north, troops openly expressed contempt for the war. Underground newspapers were printed as a counterforce to the military publication, *Stars and Stripes*. Chapters of the Vietnam Veterans Against the War sprang up in many units. Increasingly, GIs refused to follow orders that they felt were senseless or dangerous. In October, 1971, six 1st Cav soldiers at Firebase Pace on the Cambodian border refused an order to go out on night patrol because they believed it was a suicidal mission with no purpose. The entire company backed their action.[11] In the rear, soldiers refused to follow even minor regulations, particularly the ones pertaining to hair and mustache length. They dismissed directives with a shrug and asked simply, "What are they going to do...send me to Vietnam?" Fifteen years after the CIA report was suppressed, military discipline and morale had in fact fallen victim to a war built on a lie.

When he returned from Vietnam, Frank told no one how he had felt in-country. He retired from the Army as a colonel after serving another six years. He stored the pain, bitterness, anger and frustration of his tour as effectively as he closeted his four boxes of Vietnam slides. He was not unusual. Most veterans did the same. On a rainy Saturday afternoon in April, 1991, I asked him to share his story. At the time, Frank was fighting the cancer that would take his life in December, 1992. He was willing, even anxious, to talk about Vietnam and lightly suggested that God had kept him alive to tell the stories he had not shared, even with his wife, Betty.

With characteristic empathy, he said we who were in the rear had it easy, that we knew nothing about the life of the grunts. Frank was not able to reconcile what he witnessed in Vietnam with what he believed about the military. It hurt him to talk about it, but he knew exactly what he wanted to say. In Vietnam, he had dealt with his frustration and anger by focusing on those entrusted to his care. As he sat in his study twenty years later, commitment to them demanded that he tell their story.

• • • •

CHAPTER ELEVEN

* * * * * * *

"He has faith, he has hope, and then he has dope..."

He's a convoy truck-drivin' man
He shoots all the gooks that he can
Even doin' brave deeds, he's strung out on speed
He's a convoy truck drivin' man

He's an infantry ground-poundin' man
He lives with a gun in his hand
He has faith, he has hope, and then he has dope
He's an infantry ground-poundin' man

He's an artillery shell-firin' man
Loves shootin' his cannon when he can
His rushes they bloom, his cannon goes boom
He's an artillery shell-firin' man

He's a rear echelon supply man
He smokes every chance that he can
He'll always be stoned 'till the day he goes home
He's a rear echelon supply man

Song heard on Long Binh Post, 1971

Frank Chamberlin had been commander of the hospital in
An Khe for only a month when he was called to the bedside of a
young enlisted man on his staff. The GI was comatose. That afternoon, he had gone into the local village to get an illegal drug, but no
one knew for sure what he had taken. Although his friends said it was
"coke," Frank thought the soldier showed the symptoms of a heroin,
not a cocaine, overdose. "We were up a tree," he remembered. "If we
gave him the antidote for cocaine and it was heroin, it would kill him.
If we gave him the antidote for heroin and he had taken cocaine, it
would kill him." The doctors could not do an instant analysis. They
finally treated him for a heroin overdose, but it was too late. The soldier died. Later, Frank learned the Vietnamese people did not have a
word for heroin. "Maybe some GI looking at the white powder had
used the word 'coke,' and the Vietnamese had picked up the term," he
speculated. "The fellows assumed it was cocaine. They didn't think it
was dangerous or habit-forming. Then they got addicted, or they
overdosed, or both."

While opium, barbiturates, and marijuana had always been
readily available and used by U.S. soldiers in Vietnam, heroin first
appeared within weeks of the Cambodian invasion of May, 1970.[12] A
thimble-sized vial of 97% pure heroin sold for two dollars. It could
be bought anywhere in-country, in the villages (as Frank's young GI
had done), or on U.S. posts. Soldiers did not have to inject it to get
high because of the purity of the drug. They snorted it, or they removed a small amount of tobacco from a cigarette, inserted the drug,
and smoked it. Heroin, unlike marijuana, burns with no aroma. Soldiers could smoke it on-duty in front of officers and NCOs. Off-duty,
they increased the amount they used. Heroin was so inexpensive, they
did not have to alter their lifestyles to afford it. Nor did they have to
show proof-of-age to purchase it, as they did to buy hard liquor.

Frank called the abuse "situation-specific." He said, "The
story from the perspective of the troops was always the same, with
thousands of variations: boredom, disgust with the situation, and leadership that they perceived was uncaring or stupid. When those feelings were combined with the low cost and availability of drugs, they
provided a perfect set-up for what we saw. Drug use was more widespread among the young enlisted guys. They had been in the States

during the late sixties when a lot of experimentation was going on. They weren't afraid of drugs. They also perceived they had much less control over their lives than the officers did. At least officers could make it back to the bigger bases for a break."

Combat troops were as vulnerable to addiction as soldiers in support units. "Like the rest of us, infantry soldiers saw no purpose to the war," Frank explained, " Then they'd see their buddies get blown apart by a claymore mine. They turned to drugs as their only escape from a senseless situation."

General Michael Davison was one of the first senior military commanders in Vietnam to address the escalating problem. In late 1970, at the urging of two enlisted men, the commander of II Field Force set up a voluntary rehab center for drug-addicted GIs in his command. The enlisted men called it "Pioneer House." They adopted as its logo a square shield crested with a modified peace symbol and the words, "Today is the First Day of the Rest of Your Life." Before the center's founding, addicted soldiers leaving Vietnam had two options: they could break their drug habits cold-turkey, or they could smuggle a supply of heroin to the States—hiding it in hollowed-out pieces of chess sets was a popular method— and leave the country addicted.

General Davison recruited Frank in January, 1971, to run Pioneer House as well as to provide drug-education programs for command staffs in-country. The assignment surprised him. In fact, twenty years later, he shook his head with an amazement undiminished by time and remarked bluntly, "If you had told me when I went to Vietnam that I'd end up running a drug education program, I would have said you were f—ing crazy."

Pioneer House was located in a trailer on Bien Hoa Army Base. Ten soldiers at a time stayed an average of twelve days. On General Davison's orders, they came from their units without fear of punishment. Frank was the only physician on the staff; the six counselors were all former drug users. Many GIs successfully broke their habits, particularly those that left the center and immediately went home to the States. Soldiers who came early in their tours found it more difficult. Some returned to Pioneer House several times because the counselors could do nothing to change the environment which contributed to the abuse. The war was unending, military morale was at rock-bottom, drugs were plentiful, and the units had no therapists to provide support for the GIs.

Frank tried to create change. He flew regularly to commands throughout the country to talk to staff officers. "The officers on the big bases didn't know what it was like in the bush," he explained, "how different life was in an isolated camp, or what the enlisted guys were going through." When Frank and his counselors described the extent of drug abuse, no one believed him. (At the time, an estimated 26,000 to 39,000 heroin addicts were on active duty in Southeast Asia.[13]) "The response was always, 'Not here,'" recalled Frank. "But I knew the officers didn't see the drugs because they were so well hidden, not because the soldiers didn't use them. While I met with the command staff, my guys disappeared and returned with heroin they had secured in a relatively short period of time. They knew who was using it. It wasn't always the grunts in the messed-up boonie hats with little jingling things and logos on them, the beards and the beads. A lot of regular-looking soldiers used drugs." When commanders saw evidence of the extent of the problem, their response frequently was, "I'm leaving in three weeks or three months. Why should I do anything about it?" Frank found little support for his efforts among the officers. The hardest part of his job, he said, did not come from working with addicted soldiers, but rather "knowing there was a big problem out there, and we weren't doing a lot to improve it. It was futility. People just didn't want to listen."

Frank did not stop trying, but his experiences drained him. He wanted only to help the soldiers. He expected the same of others. Describing his year in Vietnam, he spoke warmly of the satisfying moments that came from working with the staff in An Khe, and he praised the counselors at Pioneer House. He was proud he had worked in uncharted territory to accomplish some good. But by the time he boarded his return flight, Frank felt he no longer knew the military. Despite great personal admiration for General Davison, he used words born of a year's frustration when he described the relationship he had with fellow officers. Frank said simply, "They thought I was crazy. I thought they were assholes."

• • • •

Frank was not the only one who understood the depth of the abuse. So did a young sergeant stationed on Long Binh. "My single overriding memory of Vietnam," he told me in 1991, "is leaving my hooch each morning and walking over an area littered with empty plastic heroin vials."[14] Incredibly, in 1971, the number of GIs requiring hospitalization for serious drug abuse problems in Vietnam was four times that of soldiers with combat injuries —20,000 as compared to 5,000.[15]

We who worked on the internal medicine wards were unaware of the statistics, but we knew only too well the most desperate, the most personal side of the drug story.

One night, we admitted a corpsman from our own staff who had overdosed on heroin. He might have died had he not been found in time by another corpsman. When he regained consciousness in our ICU, he was embarrassed. He had seen as many overdoses as the rest of us and never thought it would happen to him. The staff made no value judgment; we just felt bad for him. It was hard to think of it happening to someone who worked with us, but heroin overdoses had become so commonplace, it was not a surprise.

Even soldiers who were addicts before they came to Vietnam overdosed in-country because they were unaccustomed to the purity of the drug. Some patients made a full recovery. Others were not as lucky. Because a heroin overdose depresses the respiratory system and causes it to arrest, the length of time a soldier's brain was without oxygen determined whether he would fully recover. Some patients never did. Those we sent to nursing homes in the States for permanent custodial care. It seemed to me as many GIs went from the medical wards to nursing homes during 1971 as went home in body bags.

Our most severely addicted patient had served two additional tours in Vietnam just to maintain his habit. On admission, we had difficulty finding a decent vein in him for an IV because they all were destroyed from shooting heroin. He went to the operating room for exploratory surgery. When the surgeons opened him up, they said he looked and smelled like rotting meat. He died within hours.

Another patient arrived from the bush complaining of diarrhea, a common problem for infantry soldiers. Dysentery medications did not help him. An abdominal exam revealed a mass and he, too, went to the operating room. This time, the surgeons found an intestinal tract filled with feces. When it was removed, the fecal material weighed twenty-four pounds and spilled over the sides of a large metal washbasin. He had used narcotics for so long he could no longer pass stool. What he reported as diarrhea was the small amount of watery feces that made it around the rest of the mass. He also died.

The way the GIs took heroin contributed to their problems. One of our patients had snorted it for so long, he arrived on the ward with a hole in his nasal septum. Another dropped it in his eyelids. A third had bacterial endocarditis caused by the dirty needles he had used. Hepatitis patients who had used contaminated needles filled another ward in the hospital, and even there, they had access to drugs. One night, the supervisor on duty discovered two patients shooting-up in the bathroom off that unit.

Heroin wasn't the only drug we saw abused. The GIs took Binoctal (50mg of Amytal and 70mg of Seconal), a barbiturate used by the French for headaches. Soldiers purchased it over-the-counter in Saigon pharmacies, or they could buy as many as twenty tablets— more than enough to kill them— on the street for as little as one dollar.[16] One GI came to us strung-out on Binoctal, disoriented and shouting obscenities. Because barbiturate withdrawal is so slow, he filled the ICU with high-decibel profanity for what seemed to be several days and nights. When he recovered, he turned out to be a nice kid who apologized for his behavior.

Some patients on our ward resorted to sniffing glue from the Red Cross model airplane kits, forcing us to lock it up with the narcotics. We felt absurd doing it, but if a soldier asked for glue to put together a model, we watched him closely. We even joked about how dumb the guys were to be sniffing glue when they could buy any kind of potent drug anywhere in-country, including the hospital.

We also took care of many alcoholics. Older sergeants came to the ward in DTs (delirium tremens) caused by years of chronic alcoholism. One night, I stood in the center of the medical intensive care unit. On my left were four young enlisted men—no one older than twenty— who had drug-related problems. Three had overdosed on heroin, one was the kid on Binoctal. On my right were four ser-

geants—none younger than forty—who were in DTs. Their obscenities more than matched those from the barbiturate addict. We had
no other intensive care patients. I was furious. At 3:00 A.M. on the
other side of the earth, I was awake solely to take care of the moral
wreckage of a war that made no sense. I stood in the center of the
ward with clenched fists as I silently cried out to some invisible authority to answer my question, "Why? Why couldn't we just pack up
and go home? Why did we have to waste so many? What possible
reason could there be for continuing this?" I got no answer.

• • • •

Terry Corneil, the platoon leader, never saw his troops use
drugs in the field. "It was very simple," he said. "As soon as you're high
in the bush, you make mistakes. The potheads knew if the enemy
didn't get them, the rest of the platoon would. We needed each other."

Back at the Bien Hoa home of the 1st Cav, however, it was a
different story. One day, Terry went to get materials from resupply.
The clerk who helped him had a little plastic heroin vial—the two-
dollar model— curled up in his hair. As he leaned down to fill out the
form for Terry's supplies, the vial fell onto the counter. Terry looked
at it, then at the clerk, then back at the vial. Finally he asked, "What
the hell is that?" The soldier said, "Nothing," and put it away. Terry
walked out. That Terry Corneil virtually ignored what happened at
resupply speaks volumes about the extent of drug abuse among American soldiers. Terry admitted his silence showed poor leadership, but
justified his nonaction by saying, "What the hell, he was a REMF!"
Heroin use in the rear was so expected in 1971 that Terry was not
surprised the soldier used the drug. He was startled only by its blatant display.

• • • •

American soldiers discovered Vietnamese marijuana soon
after the first ground troops arrived in 1965. It was cheap and potent.
A half-pound of plain, pure marijuana sold for five dollars. Eventually, two addictive cultures evolved among the troops. "Juicers" drank

heavily and were usually older than "heads," who smoked marijuana. Alcohol use, of course, was legal. And it was encouraged by plentiful supplies, low prices, and acceptance by the military. Marijuana was illegal and foreign, so officers and NCOs cracked down on its use. When they did, young GIs turned to heroin to avoid detection and prosecution. By 1971, there was so much heroin addiction in Vietnam, marijuana was no longer considered the "evil weed," and had become, not legal, but socially acceptable. During his Christmas tour of 1970, Bob Hope cracked several well-received jokes about the potency of marijuana available in Vietnam. That same month, shortly after my arrival in-country, I went to a party in the hooch of a senior officer on the hospital staff. Everyone there was smoking *Park Lanes*, prerolled marijuana cigarettes that came packaged to look like commercial cigarettes in the States, right down to an official-looking seal on the pack.

Corpsman Chris Slavsky smoked pot the entire year he was in Vietnam. "We were so darn tired when we got off duty," he remembered, "we just wanted to turn off." He was not unusual; every enlisted man he knew smoked marijuana. But Chris was surprised by the widespread use of heroin. "Of the guys I knew, I'd say 50% smoked heroin, or 'scag' as they called it," he said. "It was so easy to get, I think they were into it before they realized what was happening." Many smoked heroin while they were on-duty, which bothered Chris a great deal. "When I was off, I enjoyed myself," he recalled. "But when it was work time, I didn't feel it was right, especially when we were dealing with people's lives." Though irritated, he did not tell anyone how he felt. "I wanted to protect myself," he explained. "I knew if I got too many guys on my wrong side, I'd end up with more trouble than I needed. There were so many people involved with it, there was nothing that could be done. It was too common. It was too accepted."

• • • •

For years, military inspectors had tried to stop soldiers from leaving Vietnam with drugs, but no comprehensive efforts were initiated to address the drug problem until demoralization and abuse became rampant. In January, 1971, General Creighton Abrams (successor to William Westmoreland as commander of U.S. forces in Vietnam) issued a sixty-four page directive to address the problem. The following June, the military command began a countrywide crackdown. All GIs leaving Vietnam were required to submit urine specimens for drug testing. They had to be drug-free to board "freedom birds" for home. Immediately, a black market in "clean" urine sprang up, to be thwarted by a new regulation that stipulated each person had to be watched while urinating. Many soldiers could not urinate in front of MPs, so they drank large quantities of beer to help them out. Unfortunately for them, the beer so diluted their urine that it could not be tested, and the sample was rejected. They were forced to miss the flight they had eagerly awaited for a year until they could give a concentrated enough urine sample. Other soldiers tried to overcome their hesitancy by jumping up and down, punching their kidneys to no avail. Women leaving the country were taken from the 90th Replacement Battalion to the emergency room of the 24th Evacuation Hospital where a nurse observed them urinating. When I went home in November, 1971, I was not allowed to give my specimen before leaving the 24th. An MP drove me back to the hospital with two other women after I checked-in at the 90th. Among the few souvenirs I have of my service in Vietnam is an affidavit that I had indeed been observed urinating the tested specimen.

Along with urine testing, the Army began an amnesty program for addicted soldiers who were willing to seek treatment. The 1300-bed convalescent hospital at Cam Ranh Bay became a detox center. Other branches of the service joined the effort. Chief of Naval Operations, Admiral Elmo Zumwalt, Jr., announced a thirty-day naval amnesty program during the month of June.[17] In July, 1971, the Navy and Marine Corps began a "drug exemption" policy for personnel who volunteered for rehabilitation, but commanders emphasized second-time offenders would be prosecuted.[18] The armed forces finally had begun to address the massive problem. (In 1973, Pentagon figures estimated that 35% of Army enlisted men who served in Vietnam tried heroin, and 20% were addicted to it at one point in their tours.[19]) Despite reported abuses of the urine-testing program and the availability of heroin at the detox center itself, [20] large numbers of young soldiers at

last were able to break their addictions without fear of punishment.

Little, however, could be done to control the supply of heroin.
Tentacles of the drug trade stretched too deeply into the political and
economic centers of the war to permit an exploration into its source.
This was confirmed by a May, 1971, House Foreign Relations Com-
mittee finding that corruption, which reached the highest levels of
the US-backed Laotian, Thai, and South Vietnamese governments,
effectively blocked any chance the drug trafficking might be stopped.[21]
In July, 1971, NBC reported that South Vietnamese President Thieu
was funding his reelection campaign with drug money. Thieu called
the charge shocking and slanderous.[22]

Drugs handicapped the efficiency of American troops in
Vietnam, benefiting the North Vietnamese and the Viet Cong. Frank
Chamberlin said, "I couldn't prove it one way or the other, but I'm
sure a lot of the losses we had were due to people on guard duty and
in responsible positions who were less than fully functional because
of drugs." He and his counselors alternately blamed the Soviet Union,
China, and "the mob" for getting addicts started in Vietnam so they
would carry their addictions home. Though CIA involvement in the
drug trade has always been rumored, Frank never felt high-ranking
U.S. personnel benefited from the heroin trade because, as he said,
"It's a U.S. trait to maximize earnings. The heroin was too cheap."

Eventually, the suppliers did not even charge the going two-
dollar rate. A helicopter pilot stationed at Long Binh in 1972 told me
he once saw Vietnamese men and women throwing scores of the small
plastic heroin vials over the perimeter fence onto the post.

• • • •

CHAPTER TWELVE

• • • • • • •

"The war became a people thing."

One evening, two MPs arrived on Ward 2 to talk to Stephanie Genthon. They had discovered her watch in our hoochmaid's pocket during an exit inspection at the Long Binh gate. The MPs assumed it had been stolen. "They made me go to the station with them," remembered Stephanie. "I told them I had probably just left it in my pocket, because I kept my room locked. The mamasan told them the same thing. She said she took it out to wash the uniform and forgot to replace it. The MPs wanted me to press charges. They got furious with me when I said she was telling the truth. I really thought she would have brought it back to me. They were pretty angry when they took me back to work." By refusing the MPs' demands, Stephanie earned the gratitude of the woman whose survival depended on keeping her job. "From then on, she couldn't do enough for me," Stephanie said. "Sometimes, she'd wake me up in the morning and send me to work with corn on the cob. She was a sweet lady."

• • • •

Though we lived in their land, Americans knew little of the Vietnamese people. Twenty years of U.S. policy decisions related to Vietnam were rooted in social ignorance, with almost no attention paid to those most affected by their execution. The division between us went far beyond language and cultural differences. We did not get to know the Vietnamese because ours was not an alliance of equals. Americans dictated the terms of the partnership: while we saved them from communism, the Vietnamese served us. In 1971, hundreds of thousands of Vietnamese civilians worked on U.S. bases as secretaries, cooks, hospital aides, hoochmaids, garbage collectors, shipping clerks, and waitresses.

Despite our defined roles, many individual Americans like Stephanie were able to form bonds, even friendships, with the Vietnamese in cities and villages, in orphanages and hospitals, and in our hooches. The personal connections transcended the war around us. "That was when the war became a people thing," remembered dustoff pilot, John Miller. "Once you got to know the people, it got harder and harder to figure out what the hell we were doing there destroying their country."

Every morning at eight, two Vietnamese women— one was the woman who had been picked up by the MPs— arrived at hooch #3 to collect the bags of laundry and dirty boots we put outside the doors of our rooms before going to work. They scrubbed our clothing by hand on the floor of the shower and dried it on lines and on the concertina wire that surrounded our quarters. We returned to our rooms after work to find clean, ironed clothes hanging on our doors with shined boots below them. It was always the same, dry or monsoon season. Each of us paid the women $6.80 a month and provided cleaning materials and an iron.

Like most Vietnamese women, the mamasans were very petite, but they were strong women. Scrubbing our clothes was the least of their tasks. Many were mothers, and most worked through pregnancies. When they left us at the end of a day, they took care of large extended families that they supported with their menial jobs. The war-driven inflation rate, which approached triple digits, forced women to take any position and suffer any indignity, like the daily search at the exit gate, to keep a job. Sometimes, we nurses gave the hoochmaids extra money or brought them gifts from the PX. Many times, however, it was they who helped us. We did not speak the same language, but when they patted us on the arm, or greeted us with an especially friendly smile, it was a taste of home, and we badly needed the warmth. "They were always pleasant," recalled Stephanie, "and it wasn't just the women at the hospital. It was all the Vietnamese I met. I think if someone came to the U.S. from another country and set up camp down the road from where I lived, and told me how to run my life, when I saw one of them I would say, 'Oh, God, there goes another one.' But I don't ever remember a native looking at me with the kind of disgust that I would have for somebody who camped in my country. The Vietnamese were always gracious. I don't think I would have been as gracious."

If they needed hospital care, most Vietnamese went to their own hospitals, but some were admitted to American medical facilities, most often for reconstructive surgery. During the summer of '71, a minimal care unit for Vietnamese adults and children opened in a former POW compound across the road from the 24th Evacuation Hospital. Many of the patients in the forty-bed unit had lost limbs to mines or booby traps. Others had bullet wounds or napalm burns. There were lots of babies, and children with cancer and TB. A mother, older sister or cousin stayed with the children, sleeping on woven mats under the beds and helping with nursing care. Surprisingly, the facility was open for only three months before it was abruptly closed. "We never knew what happened or where the patients went," said Chris Slavsky, who helped run it, "and they were so badly hurt."

In March, 1971, before the special unit opened, I arrived on Ward 7 to work the night shift and was shocked to find a one-month-old baby had been admitted to the unit earlier that afternoon. The little boy had neonatal hepatitis and could not have weighed more than five pounds. He was a small silent bundle in a crib large enough to hold a four-year-old. (Where the crib came from, I do not know.) Pediatrician Doug Powell—who would one day be my husband— brought the baby to the 24th from an orphanage not far from the hospital.

Doug, tall and friendly with an engaging smile, loved taking care of children. After completing his second year of a three-year pediatric residency in Houston, he had enlisted in the Army Medical Corps to avoid being drafted during his final year of training. "I also thought I would get a better assignment if I enlisted," he recalled. "The Army didn't need any more pediatricians, so they made several

of us preventive medicine officers [public health officers]. It was probably one of the smarter moves they made, because the only skill I had
from my residency that would benefit the Army in Vietnam was knowing about infectious diseases." After basic training, Doug completed a
preventive medicine course at Ft. Sam Houston and a tropical medicine program at Walter Reed Army Medical Center. He arrived in
Vietnam in February, 1971, where he became the preventive medicine officer of Long Binh Post. "I was really lucky not to be out in the
jungle like a lot of docs," he said.

Doug's official duties left him enough time to take care of
children, and he began to visit a hospital run by a French-Canadian
medical brother that was three miles from Long Binh. There, he saw
his first case of polio. "At Walter Reed, no one had mentioned polio,"
he remarked. "I didn't even know it existed in the country. Twenty
years after the Salk and Sabin vaccines, American doctors just didn't
think of polio as a possible diagnosis, and it was endemic in Vietnam.
They never mentioned leprosy, either, and I heard there was a leper
colony south of the post."

Besides visiting the Vietnamese hospital, he went regularly
to two or three orphanages run by nuns. The majority of the children
in them had been fathered by American soldiers. "They had every
imaginable combination of features," recalled Doug. "One child might
look like a typical Vietnamese child, but have red, blond, or dark curly
hair. Other kids looked more Caucasian in their features, but had
straight Asian hair. There were many adults in downtown Saigon with
the same mixed features whose fathers had been French. We heard
that when the French were defeated in 1954, they left enough money
in Vietnam for the children they had fathered to be raised to adult-
hood. Americans left their children without support, to be raised in
orphanages and on the street."

Doug, always interested in babies, spent a good deal of time
in the infant rooms at the orphanages. "They were all set up the same
way," he explained. "Twenty to thirty small metal cribs were in a room.
Unless the babies were sick, they were two to a crib, lying crosswise,
not lengthwise. Their T-shirts were clean but stained. None wore diapers. The crib bottoms were metal screens. When the babies urinated
or defecated, it went through the bottom of the crib to the floor. Viet-

namese nurses or their helpers rolled the crib aside, mopped the tiled floor, and rolled the kids back. It was efficient, and diapers didn't have to be washed. The windows only had shutters, no screens, so flies were plentiful."

He often wanted to take the sickest baby back to the 24th Evac and was surprised to meet resistance from the nuns. "They felt it was a needless expenditure of resources since so many more kids could be helped with the same amount of time and money," he remembered. "The physician in me wanted to save the child who was dying. Theirs was a whole new way of looking at things. I learned a lot from those nuns." The nuns did let Doug bring some babies to us, and the little boy with hepatitis (who recovered) became the first of many children we cared for. Often, Doug left medications at the orphanage to treat infections. When he realized that he kept seeing the same kids with the same infections, he became disillusioned and angry with the nuns. "But I discovered they sold the medicines on the black market to buy food," he said, "It was more important to eat than to get an ear infection cured. I quickly managed to get over my disillusionment."

Older children in the orphanages ranged in age from four to fifteen. "Their problems came from inadequate nutrition and a low level of hygiene," said Doug. "I treated worms, rashes, ear infections, lice, sores, impetigo, and scalp abscesses. Some of the children had lost their hearing due to chronic ear infections."

He not only made regular visits to hospitals and orphanages, he ran a weekly pediatric clinic on Long Binh for the children of American soldiers, as well as for Vietnamese children brought to him by GIs. In April, a group of U.S. naval advisors brought Hau Van Quang to Doug's clinic. He was the eleven-year-old son of a Vietnamese senior naval officer with whom they worked. Quang had leukemia. Doug admitted him to Ward 7 and started him on the chemotherapy available in-country. Everyone, particularly the GIs on the ward, loved him. When he was feeling strong, he was all over the ward playing with the guys. When he was sick, he was stoic. Like a little soldier, he held his arm rigidly straight for us to draw his blood, and he lay quietly in bed to receive transfusions. After three weeks, Quang's leukemia went into remission. Several months later, the remission ended, and a very sick child returned to us. "He had a very high fever," remembered Jan Hyche. "We sandwiched him between the cooling blankets, by physician's order, but he would cry and beg to come out. I couldn't resist and would hold him in my arms with his head on my chest. His brother and sometimes his mother would stay all night and sleep on a mat under his bed, but one of them was always at his side." Doug discharged Quang when he realized the little boy was dying. "Quang was Buddhist," he said. "His family believed that dying away from home would deny him an eternal place with his ancestors."

Doug and the U.S. advisors were invited by Quang's father to his funeral. "In the Buddhist faith," he explained, "time of burial depended on the age of the deceased. Quang's casket had to be lowered into the ground at exactly 10:00 AM. If he were younger, he'd have been buried earlier. Older, he'd have been buried later."

Doug joined the funeral procession at Quang's home and raced with it through the crowded, narrow streets of Saigon to arrive at the cemetery in time. He described the burial: "The children all wore white. Quang's brothers and one sister wore white headbands. There were lots of flowers that the children took and distributed around the cemetery, so each grave would have a flower. They were running like little kids, but they were doing it in a respectful manner. Prayers were led by a professional prayer or ceremonial leader, not a priest or monk. They were said under a canopy, then his little casket was taken to the grave where more prayers were said rather hurriedly, and the casket was lowered on time. Once Quang was in the grave and his coffin was covered up, the family broke out Cokes and beers. We all stood around the gravesite, drinking. Despite the drinking, it was very sad."

After the funeral, the family gathered with friends at their home. "There was a simple 'altar' in the living room," Doug recalled. "On it was a picture of Quang's grandfather. Next to the grandfather's photo was a picture of Quang. Some of his favorite things were there, too, so people would remember not only Quang, but the things that made him happy. In the collection was a can of Coke." Plenty of food was put out for the mourners. Quang's father introduced Doug to all of them. "He was so gracious, but I felt bad," he said, "like I had somehow failed. I really didn't want to stay around, but I knew it was important to be there for a little while."

Soon after Quang's death, the U.S. advisors and Vietnamese naval officers Doug had met through Quang's father asked him to go on med-caps (Medical Civil Action Projects: medical outreach) to local villages. U.S. military commanders began med-caps during the mid-sixties as an official effort to win the support of the Vietnamese people. In time, med-caps became voluntary, and individual doctors, dentists, nurses, and corpsmen saw them as a chance to bring medical care to the people whose country was being destroyed by war. The missions depended on the interest and available time of each health professional. Had his schedule permitted it, Doug would have gone on med-caps seven days a week. "I learned so much," he said. "I was very naive when I began to go on them. Like many Americans, when I got orders to go to Vietnam, I didn't think of it as a Third World country. We didn't even use that term then, but that's what it was."

I was one of six or eight nurses who went with Doug to some of the villages. The Vietnamese officers guided us. For safety, we never told the village in advance that we were coming. We took different routes to and from each village, and we varied the days that we went. The American naval advisors, all of whom spoke Vietnamese, came with us. We rode in an Army green panel van with a red cross on its side. One afternoon during monsoon season, the rear wheels of the van got caught in the mud on our way to a village. Everyone—four or five nurses, a couple of doctors, and the advisors — got out in the torrential rain to push it. We succeeded in dislodging it, but by the time we got to the village, we were soaked to the skin and covered with mud. Hours later, after we had seen several hundred patients, we finally dried off.

We were fortunate to work in a building during that med-cap. Another time, we visited a more rural village and set up in an outdoor meeting place with only a thatched roof over us. Dark clouds filled the sky, and a light rain began to fall. Suddenly, lightning flashed, thunder cracked, and the earth shook. Ozone filled the air. We heard a woman screaming for a "Bac Si" (doctor). Doug and two of the nurses ran to her home where they found an old man who had been struck by the lightning. "He looked dead," remembered Doug. "The odor of burning flesh filled the cottage, nauseating all of us. One of the nurses rushed to do CPR (cardiopulmonary resuscitation). As she bent down for mouth-to-mouth breathing, I stopped her. The old man was chronically ill and emaciated. I was convinced he had TB, and I didn't want anyone directly exposed to the organism. I tried external cardiac massage, but it wasn't successful."

The Vietnamese officers took Doug via gunboat to villages along the Saigon River. The Chief Nurse at the 24th Evac would not allow nurses to go with him because the areas weren't completely secure, so we missed out on the more exciting trips. "The U.S. advisors told their Vietnamese counterparts that if they showed up with a doctor, it would show the people that they had the power to bring an American doctor to their remote villages," Doug explained. "There was a bridge over the Saigon River that we passed on every trip. It was something of a symbol because the Vietnamese Navy had been able to keep it intact. Every time we went by it, the Vietnamese men pointed it out in a show of pride. One week we went out, and it had been destroyed by the VC. I remember everybody being very quiet. No one said a word. I don't think they were embarassed. I think they were just depressed because their great accomplishment was no more."

In remote regions, Doug did not see much evidence of hygiene. "It was routine for a house on the river to have a walkway out to the toilet," he said. "A person would sit on the toilet and go to the bathroom directly into the river. Twenty or thirty feet away, kids would be splashing in the water."

Doug never worried about his safety when he was on the gunboat or out in the distant villages. "When the nurses started going out with me," he said, "the chief nurse at the 24th told me I had to carry a sidearm. I kept a gun in the van, but it was never loaded. I was afraid I would shoot myself in the foot. My only real scare came one afternoon when we were on a med-cap in a village between Long Binh and Saigon. We weren't more than a mile off the main road. Suddenly, U.S. helicopters began rocketing not far from us. We immediately picked up and got out of the area. I wonder how the Vietnamese people lived for all those years with the constant threat of being hit."

The people in the villages appreciated our efforts on every trip. Hundreds of women, children, and old men showed up to be seen. Adults always waited until the kids were examined, and nobody pushed or shoved. The problems we saw were similar to those Doug had seen in the orphanages: skin rashes and abscesses, infections and diarrhea. Scores of people had been crippled by polio or injured in the war.

"Only once," remembered Doug, "did I feel I was being taken advantage of, and it had nothing to do with the Vietnamese. I received a special request from an American lieutenant colonel to go to a specific village. Before we left on the med-cap, eight nurses and I met with him in his office, which was in a French colonial villa. For half-an-hour, he briefed us on the importance of the mission. I don't remember specifically what he said because I was upset by how long it took. He stood at his desk, which was ringed by a semicircle of comfortable chairs and sofas. Because he stood, the nurses remained standing. I sat. He finished by telling us his people would be there the whole time to support us. They needed only to be told what to do."

The Americans arrived in the village shortly before noon. Word spread, and people came out by the hundreds to see them. As lines formed, the colonel's men disappeared. Doug and the nurses worked nonstop through the hottest part of the day with nothing to drink. "The Navy guys always brought a cooler of soft drinks for us," Doug said. "But that day, the people kept coming and no one was around to help us." When the soldiers returned, he and the nurses packed up and left, over the objections of the colonel's junior officers. "We were exhausted and dying from the heat," he explained.

The colonel was furious. The next day he ordered Doug to return to the village. "When he called me," Doug said, "I told him he hadn't lived up to his part of the bargain, and besides, he couldn't order me to go on a med-cap. They were voluntary, and there was no way he could order me to treat civilians. Then I hung up on him. I think what angered me the most was that he had made such a big deal of the importance of this 'mission.' Then his guys left us without any support. On every other med-cap, the people who came with us—nurses, doctors, corpsmen, translators, Navy guys—all came purely to help people. They were

people-to-people experiences. The colonel made it a military mission."

Unlike Doug, not all doctors who served in Vietnam felt med-
caps were helpful. Some disparagingly referred to them as "one-stop
medicine." They believed the health problems of the Vietnamese were
so great, people would be better off with no intervention than with
the temporary "band-aid" med-caps provided. One doctor, who served
with a 1st Cav unit in the bush, told me they were a farce. He complained that the antibiotics he gave to the villagers were passed immediately to the Viet Cong, though he did concede that people gave
away the drugs to survive. For Doug, med-caps provided a chance to
help the victims of the war, an opportunity many Americans never
had. He fondly recalls the nuns and nurses he met at the orphanages,
the Vietnamese naval officers, and the people in the villages. He re-
grets that "more Americans couldn't have gotten to know the Vietnamese people as equals rather than as our victims."

• • • •

For a variety of reasons, most Americans who served in Vietnam did not want to know the South Vietnamese people. Some ridi-
culed them for being primitive and treated them with blatantly racist
scorn, calling them "gooks" and blaming them for our being in Vietnam. Soldiers in from the bush could not trust anyone who was Vietnamese because it was impossible to tell friend from foe. GIs in the
rear preferred the security of the base to meeting people in a country
they saw as dangerous. But many Americans maintained a distance
from the Vietnamese people because they could not face the damage
being done to them and their country by Americans.

We who were in Vietnam in 1971 saw the results of seventeen years of U.S. involvement in the lives of the Vietnamese. Large
regions of the countryside and thousands of villages were destroyed.
To escape the war, millions of villagers moved from their ancestral
lands into an already congested Saigon, transforming it into a sprawling urban refugee camp. Family structure was upended, cultural values trampled. The elderly were no longer honored. Hundreds of thousands of women, some as young as thirteen years of age, turned to

prostitution to feed their families. The black market flourished, bars proliferated. Despite the good we did as individuals, our presence in their country was destroying the people we were supposed to "save." It was hard for us to accept. "Everyone knew we were destroying their country, but no one talked about it," Stephanie Genthon Kilpatrick recalled. "Everybody knew that what we were doing just didn't sit right, but nobody knew how to fix it. So, rather than have one more thing to be upset about, we just ignored it and hoped that as soon as we left, they'd be able to put their culture and beliefs back into place. Americans created the whole situation, and then we got on a plane and went home, like it wasn't real to us. The large number of Amerasian kids we left and the whole prostitution thing was part of it. Guys shacked up with women and then left. The women and their children became outcasts in their own society. What we did was wrong. But there was just so much you could handle. The rest you shut out 'cause you'd lose your mind if you didn't."

Even as U.S. troops withdrew in 1971, our abuse of the Vietnamese people continued unabated. One evening, I stopped at the 24th Evac officers' club after a very busy day of work. A rowdy group of infantry officers sat at a corner table, celebrating the impending departure of a captain in the group. The more they drank, the louder they got. As the man going home reviewed his year in Vietnam for all within earshot, he was proudest that he had impregnated three women during his tour. I had been in-country nine months and had long since grown accustomed to officers like the captain, so I wasn't surprised. Hating him, and us, I got up and left.

• • • •

CHAPTER THIRTEEN

• • • • • • • •

"We closed our eyes and we shot our brothers."

"Get away from me, gook! Don't lay your hands on me again or I'll blow your brains out!" yelled the patient on Ward 8. He punctuated his shouts with obscenities and swinging arms. Letters stacked on his bedside stand went flying. Ward activity stopped. Other patients looked in silence at the soldier just in from the bush. They knew why he wanted nothing to do with Son Dinh Nguyen, our Vietnamese orderly. I was embarrassed for Son. Attacks weren't frequent, but when someone did lash out at him, my heart broke. Son's face tightened at the GI's abuse, but he said nothing. He turned from the angry soldier, walked over to me, and suggested someone else take his blood pressure. Then he went on to the next patient. A corpsman picked up the letters from the floor. Ward activity returned to normal.

Son's response was characteristic of the way he handled everything— with quiet understanding. He knew what the GIs faced in the bush. And he knew that the only way to help our patient was to get out of his way. So he did.

Having worked for three years at the 24th Evac, Son was an integral part of the internal medicine staff. Just a few years older than most of us, he had a ready smile that matched a quick sense of humor. Son could get along with almost anyone. And since the rest of us went home after a year, he was the one person who gave the ward continuity. "I liked working with Americans," he said, "and I liked taking care of sick people."

Jan Hyche remembered, "Mr. Son was the greatest, so wonderful in many, many ways and so skilled at the jobs required of him."

After I returned to the States, I wrote to Son in care of a staff nurse at the 24th Evac. Other nurses and corpsmen who had worked with him did the same. In May, 1972, when the hospital closed, we sent letters directly to his home in a town near Long Binh.

Son sent a present when Doug and I were married in 1973 and a congratulatory card when our daughter was born.

In April, 1975, with the North Vietnamese Army at the gates of Saigon, Son, his wife, Kim, and their three-year-old daughter, Kathie, along with thousands of other Vietnamese who had worked for Americans, were to be evacuated. But in the chaos of Ton Son Nhut Airbase, the family became separated. Kim and Kathie escaped via helicopter. Son, unable to get out of Vietnam, did not see his wife and daughter for nine years.

In May, 1991, I visited the reunited Nguyen family at their home in San Jose, California. Son was the same soft-spoken man I had known in Vietnam. He freely shared his feelings about his country and about Americans. Before I went to Southeast Asia, I thought of Vietnam as a war that had been fought for too long and a place where too many Americans had died. But because of Son Dinh Nguyen as well as the villagers we met, I learned to appreciate the Vietnamese people. His story and Kim's give testimony to their strength and to the Vietnamese commitment to family. It is important to me that Americans know it.

• • • •

Son was born in Hai Duong, a rural North Vietnamese village, in 1945. World War II had just ended; the Viet Minh rebellion against the French, under the leadership of Ho Chi Minh, was just beginning. The conflict filled Son's early years. "I remember when I was a little boy," he said, "my mother throwing me into a ditch under her body to protect me from an artillery attack. In 1951, my father was killed trying to save the life of a friend during a Viet Minh attack on a section of railroad in the North."

When the Geneva Accords of 1954 partitioned Vietnam, Son's family joined almost one million predominantly Catholic northerners in an exodus to the South. President Ngo Dinh Diem's Saigon government gave the settlers forested land in the South that they cleared with hand saws and shovels. Diem pressured French rubber plantation owners to build villages (homes, a school, a church) for the Catholic northerners in return for their labor. Son's mother was one of the workers. "She rode a plantation bus to the rubber trees early each morning where she worked with the rest of the villagers until dark," he remembered. "She had to make a crescent cut in the bark of each tree and hang a small pail on it to collect sap. If she fell behind in collecting her quota, the others helped. Many days after school, I hurried to the trees to help her."

With his mother's encouragement, Son went to high school in Long Kanh, a city not far from the plantation. He and five friends from the village rented the upstairs floor of a home. "Our landlord asked us to leave when the family that lived downstairs complained about the noise we made," he recalled with a smile. "We wrestled a lot." For the remaining three-and-a-half years, he stayed with a family whose children he tutored in return for room and board. He then completed two years of college preparatory work, hoping to attend Saigon University. "I failed the admission test to the university," said Son, "because it covered six years of work. I thought it would cover material only from my preparatory classes and not include what I had studied in high school, but it did."

In 1966, at twenty-one years of age and without the protection of a student deferment, the Army of the Republic of Vietnam (ARVN) drafted Son. Like his American contemporaries, he began to pay attention to what was happening in his country only after he was in the Army. "Most teenagers think only of themselves," he explained, "so I did not know what was going on, not even when President Diem was killed in 1963. I was sad, but I did not really think about it."

Son became a sergeant in an ARVN Ranger unit that operated in the Delta, south of Saigon. Lifted by U.S. helicopters into regions of reported Viet Cong activity, the Rangers secured villages, left them in the hands of local forces, and moved on to other areas. In November, 1967, he was offered a spot in the Officers' Training School class that was scheduled to start the following January. A month before the course was to begin, a combat injury cut short his military career.

"One afternoon," he explained, "my unit was dropped into a clearing. We came under heavy fire from the VC as soon as we were out of the helicopter. A close friend of mine who was next to me, got hit. I jumped up and started firing at where the shots came from. I was hit in the head and blacked out. Many hours later, I woke up. I was still lying in the clearing. My left side was numb, and I could not move. I called to a friend who was checking bodies around me. He was so happy to see me alive." A waiting evacuation helicopter took him to an ARVN hospital in Can Tho, where he recovered. "But I was so depressed," he said. "I could only move my right arm and leg. I felt like half a man. When my family came to visit, I was upset they saw me that way, even though they were happy I was alive."

When he left the hospital, he moved into the Can Tho home of his doctor to continue carefully monitored physical therapy. "I helped the doctor's children with their schoolwork to pay for his care," recalled Son. "The doctor told me if I would follow the exercises he gave me, I would get movement back in my left arm and leg. He was right, the movement came back, but I am still numb in my left foot. When I put on my shoe, I have to look down to see what I am doing because I cannot feel it."

In late January, 1968, while still a patient, Son went on a furlough to his uncle's home in Ho Nai, not far from Long Binh Post, to celebrate the lunar New Year, or Tet, for which a U.S.-North Vietnamese truce had been declared. In a dramatic violation of it, the combined forces of the North Vietnamese Army and the Viet Cong unleashed an offensive on U.S. and ARVN bases, 108 provincial capitals and villages throughout the South. American forces found themselves fighting the enemy on the grounds of the U.S. Embassy in Saigon; the ammunition dump at Long Binh was rocketed. "It was terrible!" Son remembered. "There was gunfire everywhere! When I heard the firing, I did not know what happened. I went out into the street. There were VC there, in my own street! I wore a civilian shirt, but I had on my Army uniform pants. They didn't pay much attention to me because they were hurrying to get away. They asked me where the forest was. Right away, I pointed in the direction and said, 'That way!' They took off. We could hear fighting for about half an hour. Then we heard helicopter gunships. That ended the fighting for a while, but many people had been killed."

With the Tet offensive, the Viet Cong took the war from the jungles and rural villages to the cities and towns. Life changed for the South Vietnamese. "We were all very scared," Son said. "The war had come to us, to our town. Suddenly, we did not know what the future would bring. We might have a good day and believe everything was normal, but in the middle of the night something might happen. Everyone left their homes and went to the Catholic hospital. That's what we did up north. Anytime there was a problem, you went to the church or some other community building. There was much concern about the war."

Before joining the Rangers, Son had retaken and passed the university admission exam, so once his extremities regained movement, he applied for a medical discharge from the Army to resume his studies. He said, "I was very surprised that the Army doctors— there were ten of them who had to review my case— gave me a choice. They said I could leave the military or remain on duty at a desk job." For Son, a desk job was "women's work," so he left the army and began classes, first in Can Tho and then at Saigon University. He studied law part-time because he could study on his own time, and he applied to work on Long Binh Post.

Son scored the highest grade on the pre-employment test at the Long Binh personnel office. After completing eight weeks of training as an aide, he joined the staff of Wards 7 and 8. He and other Vietnamese aides took two-hour English lessons each morning during his first months on duty. After 130 hours of class, he became the ward interpreter.

"I worked from 8:00 AM to 6:00 PM six days a week," he explained. "When I got off, I walked to my uncle's home in Ho Nai, picked up my motorcycle, and rode to Saigon for classes [a distance of twenty miles]. Every night I came back to Ho Nai after class unless the Army closed the road. If that happened, I stayed overnight with relatives in Saigon and came back in the morning." He and Kim, whom he had first seen with her family at the Catholic hospital during Tet, were married in October, 1970. Kathie was born a year later.

In January, 1972, the 24th Evacuation Hospital downsized. Internal medicine patients were evacuated to the States, and Son went to work in the emergency room. There he acquired minor surgical skills, which helped him find work after the hospital closed. Impressed by his diverse abilities, the U.S. Defense Attaché Office hired him to run a dispensary on Long Binh Post for American and Vietnamese workers on the base.

The dispensary was a two-bed clinic in a house trailer. To stock it, Son had access to a warehouse filled with equipment from the 93rd and 24th Evacuation Hospitals. "I could pick out anything I needed," he remembered. "Because I was allowed to order any books I wanted to use, I read a lot of medical books. If I needed any medications, I submitted a requisition, which was approved by someone on the staff. If someone got sick on the job, I determined when he could return to work. I had no one telling me what to do."

During the three years he ran his "independent medical practice," three women went into labor. He took each one to a Vietnamese hospital in an Army ambulance, and stayed until they had their babies. Then he drove to tell their families where they were. "I was very proud of my work," he recalled. "I was very happy that I was the one Vietnamese aide who got such a good job."

In April, 1975, Son's world turned upside down. A North Vietnamese spring offensive swept the length of the country with surprising speed. As the NVA moved on Saigon, U.S. diplomatic personnel began a rapid evacuation. The colonel in charge of the Defense Attaché Office asked Son to draw up flight manifests (passenger lists) for the evacuation of Vietnamese who had worked with Americans. Son methodically prepared the manifests, leaving his family for the last flight. Two of the flights he scheduled left Ton Son Nhut Airbase before the situation in Saigon deteriorated into total chaos. "It was April 28 when I took my wife and daughter to Ton Son Nhut," he recalled. "We were scheduled to get a helicopter to take us to a ship off the coast. We carried a little clothing and all our important papers, including the ones I had been given by the U.S. Army. We arrived in the evening. Saigon was going crazy. We were hungry, so I left my family on the airbase while I went to get some food for us. Right after I left, an ARVN plane flew over Ton Son Nhut and dropped a bomb on it. I do not know why it was an ARVN plane. It might have been a traitor. I think it was a signal to the NVA or the VC. Suddenly, the base was rocketed. Guards closed the gates immediately. The soldiers would not let me come back in. I was locked out, and Kim and Kathie were inside without me! I stayed outside the gate until night, and then I slept at a cousin's home. I returned first thing in the morning. When the gates were opened, I ran right to the spot where I had left them. They were not there. I looked all over and could not find them. I searched all day with no luck."

The next morning, April 30, Son searched Saigon on his motorcycle. Because Ton Son Nhut had been rocketed, he thought Kim and Kathie might have been injured. So he started with the hospitals. He did a bed-to-bed check in each one. Next he went to the churches filled with families whose homes had been destroyed by fire. He found no sign of them. Meanwhile, rockets were dropping everywhere. "I was very lucky," he said. "One hit the ground five feet from me but didn't explode! The motorcycle flew out from under me. I was knocked to the ground. I was hurt, but it was mainly scratches. When I realized I was alive, I brushed myself off, jumped back on the motorcycle and took off."

Then the motorcycle ran out of gas. Because all businesses had shut down, Son's cousin gave him a tankful. Heavy rocketing continued in the vicinity of Ton Son Nhut. Late in the afternoon, the South Vietnamese government surrendered, and the firing stopped. "I went to the airbase to look around one more time," Son said, "When I still could not find Kim and Kathie, I went to our home, thinking maybe she had gone there. She had not."

"My father-in-law told me I had probably been too upset to do a thorough search, so we returned together to Saigon the next day," he remembered. "Once again, I went bed-to-bed in the hospitals. All of them were filled. The churches and temples were packed because they were the only places people could find food and water. We checked all of them. At the end of the day we left Saigon, very sad. Three days later I went back to register with the Red Cross because they were setting up a system to locate Vietnamese in the U.S. refugee camps."

The desolate man rarely left his in-laws' home. He stayed away from the house he had shared with his wife and daughter. "Kim's family helped me," he said, "and I believed that my family was still alive. That is the only thing that kept me alive." After several weeks, he learned how to repair motorcycles and bicycles and set himself up in a small store on the road to Saigon, a route traveled daily by thousands of cyclists. With only a single pump and some tubes, Son made enough money to live.

Then the Communists came to question him. "I told them I had worked with Americans, but that I had helped people," he explained. "It did no good to lie. Everyone who lived in my town knew I had worked at Long Binh. Sometimes they had seen the ambulance in front of my home. The men who questioned me said, 'OK, don't worry.'"

Soon after, Son was sent to a three-day re-education camp. "They talked to us a lot," he recalled. "They said, 'We are not going to kill people. We were enemies before, but now we are living together.'"

The South Vietnamese in the camp had to report what they had done for the previous ten years and to describe what their families had done since 1954. "I do not think they really could check," Son said. "Some people lied, but again, I told the truth. They knew already that I had worked for the Americans. I told them that I took care of anyone who had an injury. It did not matter to me if he was a VC, an NVA, or an American. The Communists allowed each of us to keep up to 200 piastres (Vietnamese unit of currency). They took everything else and said they would hold it for us. If we needed money for something special, like a wedding, we could request it by turning in a list of expenses. They got to approve or disapprove what you were spending. They also wanted to know everything you were doing, who was coming to your house, where you were going. They wanted to know how much money you made, or, if you had pigs or chickens, how many you owned."

Every week, village residents were required to attend a propaganda meeting. "They bragged about being victorious over a big country," Son recalled. "They told us all they planned to do for us. It

was a lot of lies. It became boring. No one paid attention to them."
Except for requiring him to attend meetings, the authorities ignored
Son until he tried to escape.

• • • •

Kim Nguyen was twenty-two years old when she went with
her husband to Ton Son Nhut to be evacuated from Vietnam. She
had always depended on him or her parents to make decisions for
her. Suddenly, Son was gone, and rockets were exploding around her.
"I was sure Kathie and I were going to be killed, until the officials
moved us to a part of the base that was safer," she remembered. "When
Son did not come back to us by night, I told them I wanted to go to
my village. They would not let me leave. The next morning, we ran
back to where Son had left us, and we did not see him. Somehow, we
missed each other." All day, helicopters filled with panicky Americans
and Vietnamese departed from Ton Son Nhut and the U.S. Embassy
in Saigon. With the NVA descending on the city, no one was able to
predict how long the flights would continue. "Finally," she said, "late
in the afternoon of April 29th, I could not wait any longer and I got
on a helicopter. I did not know what to do but hope Son had gotten
on another one. I carried Kathie and a small bag of documents. I had
to throw all our clothes away."

The young mother and her tiny daughter were taken off-
shore to join thousands of refugees on U.S. ships in the South China
Sea. Kim watched hundreds of crowded fishing junks swamped by
the huge ocean vessels and wondered what was going to happen to
her. "I was very scared and alone," she recalled. "I did not speak much
English. I met a friend of Son's who helped me look all over the ship
for him. When I did not find him, I still did not lose hope. There were
many ships with refugees. I thought maybe Son was on another one."

The ship took them to Guam where they were given food
and shelter. Every time a ship or a plane arrived, Kim went to meet it,
hoping her husband was on it. "I was supposed to board a flight for
the States, but I kept asking to stay," she said. "They told me they had
to make room for more refugees who were coming." Finally, with no
other choice, she flew to Ft. Chafee, Arkansas.

There, Kim continued her search through a central registry that listed the names of refugees staying at four hastily-established camps in the U.S. "I was so happy when I found a list with Son's name on it," she said, "but it turned out to be someone else. A week after I arrived, a Red Cross telegram told me he was alive in Vietnam. I wanted to return to my country, but a priest in the camp read my palm and told me not to." She accepted sponsorship by a Catholic church in Chicago.

Several weeks later, she and Kathie began their new life in the United States. She had to secure food and shelter, learn to live in a foreign land, speak a new language, raise her daughter, then four years old, and try to rejoin her husband. Despite a rocky start, she managed it all. "Things did not work out well in Chicago," she explained, "so Kathie and I moved to Quincy, Illinois. It was a small town and people were very good to me. I found someone to watch Kathie. I lived downtown and worked in an electronics factory. After a year, I sent word to Son that I was alive. I could not do it before then because the communication between the U.S. and Vietnam had not been good. I also worried that I would cause trouble for him. So I wrote to a friend and sent Son a message in the letter. That was 1976. Until he received that message, he did not know Kathie and I were alive."

· · · ·

"I was so happy," said Son. "From the moment I heard about them, I knew I had to go to them." Through quiet investigation, he located a fisherman in Vung Tau, a coastal city east of Saigon, who owned a boat suitable for ocean travel. "I wore disguises and went roundabout ways to visit the man," Son explained. "He charged me a fee for passage that he based on the cost of gas and food, what his ship was worth, and what he would lose if we got caught. He would lose his boat and all his income. He decided where to go based on the weather, the wind, and how deep the ocean was. He thought about five countries." The shortest trip was to Thailand, but the route went through Cambodian waters, and the former North Vietnamese Army had taken over Cambodia. Malaysia was no good because of the deep ocean and strong winds. Going to Hong Kong meant going past North

Vietnam, and the captain worried about their naval vessels. The Philippines were too far away. Indonesia was the straightest course, and
there was not much deep ocean to cross. So, he chose this route. The
boat was to pick up the refugees upriver from coastal Vung Tau. "We
were huddled in the dark by the riverbank, men, women and children," Son recalled. "We planned to board quietly and go down river
into the South China Sea. When the fishing boat came near the shore,
lights suddenly went on around us. The police had learned of our
plan! They surrounded us. They would not let anyone out, even
women and little kids."

From the river, the captain, accompanied by his son, saw the
lights and heard crying. He realized what had happened, turned the
boat around and made his escape. "They were the only two people on
that boat," Son remembered bitterly. "His wife and three more children were with us."

Authorities sent Son to a farm camp not far from Vung Tau.
"Every day," he said, "whether it rained or the sun shone, I worked in
the fields growing potatoes, vegetables, and rice. And I raised pigs
and chickens. We ate the food grown in the camp, which was good
because all over Vietnam, people were starving because the whole
rice crop was sent to China to pay war debts."

Son estimated there were two hundred men with him. "At
night we slept in a building with a metal roof. We had no beds or
bunks. We slept on a wooden platform a few inches off the ground.
We were one body right next to the other. We all had manacles with
loops on our ankles and every night, they put a bar through all the
loops to hold us together when we slept."

He spent a year and a half in the camp. When he was released, the officer in charge asked Son if he would try to escape again.
Without hesitation, he answered, "Yes, as long as my wife and child
are alive, I have to go to them." The official said, "I agree. I am sorry,
but the law is the law. Just do not try to escape from my district if you
do it again."

When Son returned to Ho Nai, he worked as a wedding pho-
tographer. A friend, who developed and printed his pictures, paid
him a commission. Son enjoyed photography and was able to make
enough to support himself, but he kept looking to leave Vietnam.

After several months, he learned his brother-in-law's uncle planned an ocean escape to Indonesia. "Because he was my relative," Son said, "I could go with him for free. I promised that I would pay the fare when I joined my wife in the United States." Son was careful to plan his second escape for the delta area south of Saigon rather than the Vung Tau district east of Saigon. It placed him outside the territory of the officer who had released him from prison.

The second attempt was even more terrifying than the first. "Twenty-five people boarded the boat and we went out into the ocean," recalled Son. "At night, a storm hit. It was very windy. The captain could not handle the wheel. He was scared and even started to cry. Everyone was crying. The boat was pitching up and down in the waves. Every time it went down, a wall of water washed over us. I knew we were going to die in that boat. I was ready to die. I prayed a lot. Then I passed out, or maybe I was just so tired I fell asleep. When I woke up, the sun was out. The ocean was calm. We tried to go again. Then the wind came up, and the captain could not handle the boat. He told us he only had the boat for three months. Everyone was shocked. We had to return to Vietnam. We arrived on a small island at nine or ten at night. None of us knew which island it was since it was dark. Everyone was exhausted and we slept together on the shore. At sunrise, the police came. They caught us. They took our money, jewelry and watches. When they asked why I had done it again, I told the truth. As long as my wife and daughter were alive, I had to go to them. The police told me they understood, but I had broken the law. I was sent to another camp,"

Son spent nine months in the second camp, where the work was grueling. "Guards woke me up before sunrise each morning to work all day," he remembered. "I had to take mud from the river and mold it into bricks. I put them in front of a fire for twenty-four hours and then I put them outside in the sun to finish drying. If it started to rain, the guards rang a bell and we raced to bring in the bricks we had made. If it did not rain, each brick took four or five days to dry."

Son still has no idea how long he would have been kept in the camp were it not for the intervention of Kim's family. "My mother-in-law had relatives who had stayed up North when the rest of the family left [in 1954]. Her uncle was an NVA general. She asked him to write to the camp authorities. He told them I was his nephew, that my family was in the United States, and that I had an obligation to join them. He also told them that I had a passport and a visa. I applied for them before I tried to escape the second time. When the documents did not come through, I thought there was no hope, so I tried the escape. They came through while I was in prison but no one told me." After his release, he went to the police station to get his papers, only to discover the visa had expired four months earlier. "I was so sad," he remembered. "My second escape had not been necessary. I had spent nine months in the camp when I could have gotten out of the country legally. Now I had no visa. The authorities knew I was in the camp. They could have reached me."

He learned that replacing the visa might take two years, and there was no guarantee it would come through a second time. Desperate, Son contacted the general in Hanoi who spoke to an influential friend. "I was so grateful. He really helped me," Son said. "He told his friend I had to be with my wife and baby. He said I had made a mistake and that anyone can make a mistake." After Son gave gifts to the authorities—a stereo and toys for their children— they extended his documents for three months.

He immediately filed for U.S. immigration at the UN refugee center in Ho Chi Minh City (Saigon). The American representative, surprised that the visa had been extended, placed Son's name on a waiting list. Six weeks later, he was directed to report to the airport. "They told each of us where to sit," Son recalled. "Everyone was so quiet. While we waited, an official walked up to one family. He pointed at them and said, 'I want to see you in my office.' They followed him. We did not see them again. We were all afraid that would happen to us."

Several hours passed before the anxious travelers boarded the plane, a Boeing 707 that belonged to the Vietnamese government. Son said, "I thought maybe it would fly around and then come back down in Vietnam. I could not believe I was finally getting out of the country after all I had been through. We flew for two hours. When we landed, I saw Thai words on the sign. Bangkok! We were in Bangkok! I thought, 'Oh my God, I cannot believe it.'"

The Thai police informed him that while he no longer belonged to the Vietnamese, the Americans had yet to accept him. He spent ten days in a refugee camp before he saw a U.S. representative. With Son at his desk, the official called Kim to make sure she was still willing to sponsor her husband and pay his airfare. "Kim said 'yes,'" recalled Son, "but at another desk, I saw a lady whose husband said 'no' when the official called. He had changed his mind and did not want her to come to America. I think they sent her anyway, but she had to promise not to contact him."

On a bitter cold day in December, 1984, Kim and Kathie traveled to Chicago's O'Hare Airport to resume a relationship that had been severed nine years earlier at Ton Son Nhut. Kim was an American citizen who spoke fluent English, was employed, owned a car and had saved sufficient money to sponsor Son's immigration. Kathie was a thirteen-year-old coming to O'Hare to meet a father she did not know.

Son did not see them until they called to him. "Oh, I was so happy," he said. "There they were in front of me. I could not believe it."

"When he came off the plane," Kim said, "he looked so weak. His skin was in very bad shape. He hardly looked like the man I had known. But Kathie and I were so happy to see him."

Cultural adjustment was difficult for the man who had survived so many trials. "It was very hard," Son explained, "to accept the changes in my family. In Vietnam, I made all the decisions. In the U.S. it is different. I had to learn to listen to Kim and Kathie. My daughter was thirteen years old when I came here. It was very hard for her and for me. I wanted to use the old rules, the rules of my country. We had many arguments. But then a friend told me Kathie was an American, and since things were different here, maybe I should change."

The weather also discouraged him. "I was so cold, and I could do nothing," he explained. "I could not even go to the grocery store because I did not drive, and even if I could drive, I did not know what to buy." At Kim's suggestion, he visited an uncle who lived in the expanding Vietnamese community of San Jose. There, he saw an alternative to living in a cold climate. Within weeks, the family packed their possessions and traveled west.

In San Jose, Son has heard young Vietnamese men advocate military action to reclaim by force that which they once had, or imagine they once had in their country. "They do not know war," he said. "They have been rich in America, and their lives have been peaceful." Like them, he is bitter about what the Communists have done to Vietnam. But he expects the leaders will change. "From the time they took over the country until now is what is important," he explained. "Not what went on before. What have they done for their country? Why are the people still poor? The party will realize it is the old people, the old Communists in charge of the country until now, who have clung to an old way which does not work. The new style will mostly follow Russia. They will realize the way to change is economic. But if they change right now, it will look like they are following someone else. They want to do it their own way, in their own time, but they will change."

Son believes the United States carries a heavy burden of responsibility for what happened in Vietnam. He said, "America, Russia, and China should have left the small country alone. They should have fought each other if they were enemies and not involve us. We were told that we had to fight or we would lose our land. Back then the Americans promised everything. They said they would build our country like they had helped the Philippines and Japan. We believed them. We realized that we may fight and die, but that life for the next generation would be prosperous and peaceful. So we closed our eyes and we shot our brothers. It was not a good reason to fight. If we had won, Americans would have helped us with their high technology. We had quality resources in Vietnam. We needed development help. If we had won, companies would have come to Vietnam, Americans would have rented the ports for ninety-nine years. There would be the prosperity they promised. But Americans played games. They wanted to control everything. They gave us money so they could give the orders. When you fight, there is no time to plant, harvest, or develop. No company will invest in you because it is unsafe. No resources get developed. We became dependent on U.S. money."

"When the U.S. left my country," he continued, "it was like leaving a child alone in a shopping mall, a child who had never been left alone. The child had done everything the U.S. had asked. If he wanted to fix something to eat, the U.S. said, 'No, I will get it for you.' Suddenly, after all that time, all that money, and the great loss of life, the U.S. was no longer there. The United States should answer for what it did in Vietnam. When Saddam Hussein lost the Gulf War, the UN demanded he restore Kuwait. The Iraqis were told to rebuild everything they destroyed. The U.S. lost in Vietnam. They should help the country rebuild. They promised us everything."

Son voiced these impressions with weariness. His interest in global events is tempered by a pragmatism central to the Vietnamese character. Years of listening to political rhetoric and seeing its effect on his people have made him a cautious witness to history.

His story and Kim's bear witness to the values that allowed their ancestors to survive thousands of years of foreign domination. For both of them, the only thing that is lasting and worth dying for is the family.

• • • •

CHAPTER FOURTEEN

• • • • • • • •

"...in this mecca of political bullshit."

"The hardest part of the year was the middle of it," recalled Stephanie Genthon Kilpatrick. "I had been there so long that I couldn't remember not being there. I had so long to go, I couldn't imagine getting to leave. My whole life had become that little hospital quadrangle. To hit 'hump day' and realize I had exactly the same time left was awful. I felt like I was doomed to the dungeon for life."

My feelings were similar to Stephanie's. My early letters home were written weekly and included minute descriptions of my new life as well as requests for items I could not get in Vietnam—specific brands of shampoo, creme rinse, deodorant and tampons. I loved what I was doing, and I expressed a guarded optimism that the year would go well. "I can't tell you how happy I am at work," I wrote to my parents on December 14th. "It's the combination of working with a super fine staff, wonderful patients and being in internal medicine, the field I like. I have learned so much. I only hope it continues."

By May, 1971— my halfway point— my letters were brief and many of them started with "I'm sorry I haven't written..." Like Stephanie, it did not seem possible to me that a world existed outside of Vietnam, nor did I care. I even stopped reading my Sunday *New York Times*. Nursing satisfaction gave way to exhaustion. In late May, I wrote to a friend, "I'm tired of the same old problems, the endless stream of patients, and the hard work. I'm tired of being a nurse. I find myself snapping at the patients right and left. Oh, I have to get out!"

Events of 1971—the closing of Army hospitals, the piecemeal withdrawal of U.S. forces, the Vietnamese national elections and the nagging suspicion that the U.S. might never leave Vietnam—contributed to my distress. Between August, 1970, and December, 1971, twelve Army hospitals closed, significantly increasing our workload. After the 93rd Evac and the 12th Evac pulled out, the 24th was the only hospital left in the region immediately north of Saigon. At first, doctors, nurses, and corpsmen from those hospitals joined our staff, but when they went home, they were not replaced. Drug testing that began in June further depleted the staff: that month, forty-five corpsmen left the 24th Evac to run urine checkpoints throughout the country. In July, the internal medicine unit expanded from two to six wards, including a six-bed cardiac care unit. During the summer rainy season and therefore the malaria season, every letter I wrote included some form of "they can't work us any harder than they are."

The piecemeal withdrawal of US forces worried us. We were concerned not only for our personal welfare, but for the safety of the soldiers in the bush. In a letter to my parents I said, "I can't believe we're pulling out as we are. 'Pulling out' seems to mean no replacements of weapons, equipment, or men for the units left here. The ones in the bush have nothing. They're still expected to do the job they were doing before, with half the resources... I'm so happy I'm not up north. The nurses are sending down stories of working in flak jackets and helmets...If we don't get out of here soon, we're really going to get ourselves kicked badly."

The Vietnamese national election of late 1971 was a sham of democracy and demonstrated to us the uselessness of the cause for which so many Americans had given their lives. In September, President Nguyen Van Thieu forced his two opponents to drop out of the presidential race and used the national police to brutally smash demonstrations against him. Vietnamese who opposed him blamed the American government for his abuses. They attacked GIs in Saigon and burned American cars. We were restricted to base and put on alert during the election. At the time, we were unaware that the U.S.

Army had prepared a contingency plan to fight its way out of Vietnam not only against North Vietnamese forces, but against the South
Vietnamese who might turn on us.[23] I had just returned from an
"R&R" in Bangkok when I wrote in disgust: "Well, here I am, back in
this mecca of political bullshit. I never wanted to stay away from some-
place so much—even when I first came. It suddenly hits you when
you find yourself tromping through the mud, taking cold showers in
brown water, and working these insane hours. Then you hear about
what's going on in this country and you wonder what in hell you're
doing here. I'm so grateful I'm not in Saigon. Before this mockery of
democracy is over, all hell is going to break loose. Even the most tough-
ened GI is staying out of Saigon from now on. The week after elections will be just as unsure as the week before. Oh, how I wish we'd
get out of here!"

    But post gossip, as well as official announcements, led us to
believe the United States would never leave Vietnam. In early April,
our commanding officer told us he expected the 24th Evacuation
Hospital to become the U.S. Army Hospital, Long Binh or the South
Vietnam Army Medical Center. To prepare for the hospital's expanded
future, he oversaw the construction of two private rooms on Ward 5
for officers of field-grade rank (majors and above) as well as other
VIPs. At the request of the Chief of Medicine, he ordered state-of-
the-art monitors for our cardiac care unit, even as the quonset hut
roofs leaked. The monitors arrived in January, 1972, the month that
the 24th closed. They were never used.

    In July, an engineer friend of mine told me he had seen plans
to landscape the road leading to USARV headquarters and to con-
struct a twelve-lane, air-conditioned bowling alley, large theater, golf
course, French restaurant and PX extension at Long Binh. In October, a small convenience store opened on post. It carried fresh loaves
of bread and cartons of milk. Everyone believed it was just a matter
of time before the first fast-food hamburger franchise or pancake
house would appear on the base. I wrote bitterly, "Snow will come to
Vietnam before we go home."

    In addition to sprucing up the post, commanders at Long
Binh tried to spruce up the troops by turning their attention to military minutiae. Anyone using the PX had to be in complete uniform,

including infantry soldiers. The poor GIs who hitched helicopter and jeep rides in from the bush found they could not enter the PX if they did not wear hats or have the correct insignia on their fatigues. At the 24th, the chief nurse ordered us to keep our hair off the collars of our fatigues instead of just pulling it back, and the hospital commanding officer issued new regulations regarding our off-duty activities. Cook-outs at the officers' club were canceled ("illegal" he said), "Hail and Farewell" parties—for newcomers and staff going home— became reservation-only affairs without live music (also "illegal"), and most upsetting of all, vehicles with red crosses could no longer be used to transport alcoholic beverages (against the Geneva Convention)!

We struck back at the system in small, individual ways, but no one succeeded quite like Jan Hyche, my friend from internal medicine. She had one day remaining at the 24th Evacuation Hospital before she was to go to the 90th Replacement Battalion and home. Since anyone as "short" as Jan did not have to work on the ward, she attended an afternoon USO production in the hospital quadrangle. The show was drawing to a close when the emcee, looking out at the sea of faces before him, lighted on Jan, the only woman in the audience. He asked her to join him on stage. Jan did. As soon as she was next to him, the emcee shoved a microphone into her face and said with a big smile, "Now lieutenant, tell us your name and where you're from!" Jan smiled and sweetly said, "I'm Jan Hyche, I'm from Alabama, and the Army sucks!" The startled man kept the microphone before her and said, "I beg your pardon??" Without skipping a beat, Jan repeated, "I'm Jan Hyche, I'm from Alabama, and the Army sucks!" Patients in the audience leaped to their feet, many stood on the benches, stomping and cheering wildly. Jan had done more to lift their morale than any number of USO shows. That night she received an award at the officers' club.

• • • •

CHAPTER FIFTEEN

• • • • • • • •

"Actually, we were surprised that it hadn't dissolved the boot!"

"One night, soon after the dustoff unit returned to Long Binh," remembered John Miller, "we celebrated a pilot's DEROS with some of the nurses from the 24th Evac at an outdoor steak dinner. The nurses borrowed a huge pot from the hospital mess hall to mix 'Cu Chi Punch,' a recipe we brought back with us from Cu Chi. It was made with a variety of ingredients—not always the same— including gin, vodka, and ruby red port. It had bits of fruit for texture, and when they were available, we threw in whole jars of Maraschino cherries. We always added Tang because after all, it was what the astronauts took to the moon. The punch never put anyone on the moon, but it was guaranteed to make all of us forget we were in Vietnam! Anyway, at the party, we suddenly realized that the Long Binh curfew had passed, and we had to move our celebration indoors. So, all of us—there must have been twenty of us— piled into the back of a two-and-a-half-ton truck, put the big pot of punch in the center of the truckbed, and took off for phase two of the party. Down the road, we came across an infantry soldier hitching a ride. The truck was so high that two of the guys had to reach down to help hoist the soldier up over the railing. Well, he got a little too much help, because when he landed, one Army-green leg shod with one Army-issue jungle boot went right into the pot. That was a crowd-pleaser, needless to say. Soon, undaunted, we toasted the hysterical moment with the very same punch. Actually, we were surprised that it hadn't dissolved the boot!"

It is difficult to explain how we could have had such fun in the middle of a war. In a September letter to my mother, who was concerned about the hard work I was doing, I wrote, "Yes, Mom, I am having a good time here. I guess, even with the long hours, the hard work, and the lousy war, the people are so great and there is such a spirit, it's hard not to enjoy yourself when you're not working."

We were all in our early 20's and partying was the only legal way to escape from the hard work, the lousy war, and the political bullshit. At a moment's notice, and for any reason, we pulled together dinners using food from the PX and the mess hall. We raided hooches to see if items from care packages had been left in the community rooms. One night we prepared a spaghetti sauce using yellowed packets of seasoning that must have been around for as long as the 24th had been! With enough wine added to it, the sauce was delicious. "Cu Chi Punch" was not the only alcohol that fueled our parties.

Three nights before Christmas, 1970, the nurses from Wards 7 and 8 cooked a turkey dinner with dressing, potatoes, gravy, corn on the cob and salad for a staff party. Most of the food came from the mess hall, and we were able to prepare it when the kitchens were not being used. Operating room technicians, using sterile needles, sutured the birds for us. A week later, the hospital officers' club, which usually did not serve food, welcomed 1971 with a buffet dinner, free champagne, noisemakers, hats, a Vietnamese rock group, and a breakfast of bacon and eggs at 1:00 AM. In the midst of the gaiety, there was a strong undercurrent of hope that maybe, just maybe, this would be the year that the United States would leave Vietnam. When the rock group played the Animals' *We Gotta Get Out of This Place*, we sang it with gusto unmatched during my entire year in-country.

Like us, the most senior officers stationed on Long Binh found an escape from the war, but they did it somewhat more graciously. One night, I went as a guest to a party at the home of a general. Before dinner, we had cocktails and hors d'oeuvres on the porch of his small cottage. A low fence surrounded it, high enough to obscure the ugly post, but not tall enough to block our view of the beautiful Vietnamese sunset. The eight women at the party—I was the only nurse— wore dresses, the men wore uniforms. Enlisted men in short white waistcoats served dinner. To work in the general's mess they had to have received a Purple Heart. The china and crystal were Noritake, the tablecloth was white linen, and the napkins seemed to me to be at least two feet square.

After the dinner, we moved to the general's briefing room to watch the movie *Funny Girl*. The whole night, no one mentioned the war. The next day, I went back to work and to reality.

Another evening, John Miller and I went to see *The Fantasticks* in an auditorium at USARV Headquarters. A soldier from New Jersey who had been a patient on Ward 8 was a member of the theater troupe — remarkably, his sole assignment in Vietnam. He had given me complimentary tickets. The production was every bit as good as the one I had seen years before in New York.

In August, 1971, it was hard for me to remember that a war was going on in Vietnam when I spent a week at the Australian hospital in Vung Tau, the coastal resort city east of Saigon. The chief nurse at the 24th Evac had negotiated an exchange program with the Australians to give two staff nurses per week an in-country "R&R." I went the second week of the program. After hospital rounds each morning, we were allowed to spend the day anyway we liked— at the beach or pool, visiting ruins in the countryside, or shopping in town. At the hospital, everyone broke for coffee and small sandwiches at 10:00. Lunch, followed by a quick siesta, was from 12:00 to 1:30. Cocktails were at 6:00. Then came dinner— to which women had to wear skirts — and a movie, and more drinking at the officers' club. The club, furnished in white wicker, sat on a bluff overlooking white sandy beaches and the South China Sea. "This whole place is like a scene from South Pacific," I wrote to a friend.

Sometimes though, even when we tried to escape, it was difficult to avoid the reality that we faced every day. Stephanie Genthon Kilpatrick recalled the movie *M*A*S*H* playing to a standing-room-only audience at the 24th. "It was on for two nights," she said. "I had seen it at Ft. Lewis and remembered it had been hilarious. At the 24th, no one around me laughed. No one spoke when it was over. We all went back to our rooms without talking."

• • • •

CHAPTER SIXTEEN

• • • • • • • •

"In that case, give me a Bud."

One day, a pilot from the First Cavalry arrived at the 24th Evac Officers' Club and asked for the house brand of scotch, Johnny Walker Black Label. The bartender answered, "I'm out of Black Label. I only have Chivas Regal." The pilot responded, "In that case, give me a Bud."

Those of us assigned to Long Binh in 1971 had access to amenities GIs in the bush had long since forgotten. The sprawling base was home to many support commands —engineering, military police, aviation, quartermaster, signal—and every one of them had a club for officers, NCOs, and enlisted men. In all, there were forty clubs on the base. The larger ones—the largest was the USARV officers' club— served steak and lobster tails and had live entertainment every night. Smaller clubs, including the one at the 24th Evacuation Hospital, were nothing more than bars furnished with old upholstered furniture, tables and chairs. At the 24th, we were lucky to have a piano. In all the clubs, alcohol was plentiful and inexpensive and the consumption of lots of it was socially acceptable. A shot of premium liquor sold for twenty-five cents. Beer was ten cents. Our tastes, honed on the finest brands, grew as jaded as the pilot's.

The clubs were a major industry, and the NCOs who ran them had one job: to maintain a profitable, well-stocked operation that kept rear-echelon soldiers and their officers happy. Each one of them tried to tap into the Army supply network before anyone else knew what was in-country. The abundant supplies available, the low overhead in running a club, and the high profit margin created problems, however, because club management was limited by how much they could take in. Everything above a net gain of one dollar had to be given back to the soldiers,[24] forcing the sergeants to come up with creative ways to return the monthly earnings to the troops. In even the smallest units, club sergeants arranged for Vietnamese or Filipino bands and entertainers,— all singing heavily-accented songs like *Yellow Re-e-e-ver*— nickel beer nights, and inexpensive steak dinners cooked on outdoor grills. At one NCO club on Long Binh, the sergeant used profits to throw a party at which he showed every porno movie in-country, twenty-seven of them, each one about five minutes long. Other units had strippers entertain them.

The sergeants had such total power, and so much money crossed hands, the system begged for abuse. In 1971, a U.S. Senate investigation exposed a group of senior NCOs who had managed clubs in the Saigon, Long Binh and Chu Lai areas during the war's early years and had made thousands of dollars in kickbacks for purchases of refrigerators, furniture, liquor, and food.[25]

In addition to the forty clubs, Long Binh had six post exchanges. The largest was a corrugated steel warehouse close to the 24th Evac — a true "one-stop shopping" experience. It stocked everything from clothing, personal toiletries and snack foods, to liquor, stereos, cameras and watches. It carried bread—oval, unsliced and dry— that came in cans. The potato chips— not packaged for the humidity-laden tropics—could easily be bent in half without being broken. There was always a large supply of alcohol, beer and wine on the shelves of the exchange, but the availability of particular brands varied, so we had to stock up on what we wanted when we saw it. The same was true of cigarettes. Alcohol at the PX was as inexpensive as at the clubs. A quart of Gordon's gin sold for $1.25, Johnny Walker Black Label scotch for $4.00 and Jack Daniels for $3.20, all one-fourth to one-third of their stateside cost. To avoid a shortage, we were issued monthly ration cards for beer, wine, alcohol and tobacco. GIs who were under twenty-one years of age, even though they made up the majority of troops in the bush, could only buy 3.2% beer with their ration cards. Elsewhere on post, of course, they could buy heroin, unrationed and without proof of age.

We could even order new cars at the exchange. Auto company representatives offered a flat twenty-percent discount and arranged to ship the cars directly to our homes after our return to the States. A nurse who lived across from me in hooch #3 was saving her entire salary so she and her pilot husband could purchase a Mercedes-Benz.

If we could not find a specialty item at the PX, we ordered through the PACEX (Pacific Exchange) catalog, our passport to conspicuous consumption. The glossy color catalog, half-an-inch thick, offered an array of appliances and stereo equipment, furniture, silver, crystal, china, and jewelry. We had the items sent to us in Vietnam to avoid paying customs fees. When we left the country, they were shipped home, free of charge.

At the PX, we paid for our purchases with a military scrip—Military Payment Certificates or MPCs. The MPCs, which looked like play money, were the only legal currency American servicemen and women could use on bases in Vietnam. When they were introduced in August, 1965, MPCs were restricted to Americans. But a December, 1967, change in the regulation gave the Vietnamese the right to deal in them. Through military scrip, the local economy gained access to U.S. dollars and supplies. Inflation skyrocketed, and the black market thrived. Goods earmarked for the PX showed up in the street corner markets of Saigon where sidewalk entrepreneurs laid out their wares on the ground. Everything seen on U.S. bases made it to the black market, from shaving creme and soap to appliances and furniture.

The MPCs replaced nickels, dimes and quarters as well as dollars, so we all walked around with great wads of bills in our fatigue pockets. Because we had to convert our money as soon as we arrived in-country, the sound of jingling coins became a distant memory for us. One night, the operating room at the 24th ran out of blood, and a group of GIs who had just arrived in Vietnam came to donate. After donating, they offered to pay for cans of pop in the emergency room and asked where to put their money. A nurse told them to throw it into the collection box. She turned her head to work on a patient and suddenly heard coins being tossed into the box! The soldiers were so new in-country, they had not yet had a chance to exchange their money. The ER staff crowded 'round to look at the coins, and passed the word for anyone else on the staff who wanted to come to view them. It did not take much to have a "happening" at the 24th Evac!

On Long Binh, we could choose to eat in any of the sixty mess halls on post, at the clubs, or at one of four white hot dog trucks run by Korean vendors. One of the trucks, dubbed the "Roach Coach," stayed next to the 24th Evac's pharmacy. It opened each morning at 9:30, and served hot dogs with a choice of onions, relish, ketchup and mustard for lunch or dinner and even breakfast. Today, I shudder to think of the number of hot dogs I ate for breakfast.

The best place to eat on the base was the *Mandarin House*, a Chinese restaurant. The dim light, Chinese decor and music, delicious Asian food, and steamed, lilac-scented towels allowed us to briefly forget the ugly world outside its doors. The restaurant was privately managed under a contract put out for bid by USARV every two years. In 1971, the proprietors were two Chinese men from Cholon, the Chinese suburb of Saigon, and two Vietnamese men, one of whom had been educated at Cornell and Michigan State Universities as well as in Paris.

To insure that our food was prepared under sanitary conditions, eight enlisted men from Doug Powell's preventive medicine unit inspected the clubs, mess halls, hot dog coaches and the *Mandarin House* regularly. They also tested the safety of our drinking water, monitored the chlorine level of the eight swimming pools on post, and inspected Long Binh's twenty barber shops, one beauty shop, and the single massage parlor on post.

Doug's staff carried out their mundane duties with little attention from the USARV brass. In early October, however, senior officers became deeply interested when they awarded the two-year *Mandarin House* contract to a group of Korean businessmen. Doug's unit had to insure that the new food handlers had physical exams and certificates before the restaurant could open under the new management. "I was particularly concerned," he said, "because the new manager's last contract had been to run the hot dog trucks and he couldn't even keep them clean without close supervision. And I had

heard that the Korean businessmen were already running a shaky restaurant in DaNang. So I set up a timetable for physical exams. No
one showed up. A few days before the restaurant was scheduled to
reopen, I got a call from USARV headquarters demanding the restaurant open on time. I told the colonel I was sorry, but it couldn't.
Whoever it was got very angry. I was surprised because someone way
above me was paying an awful lot of attention to what was a relatively
insignificant matter. When I explained that no one had gotten the
required physicals, I got some results. Workers started to dribble in,
but the pressure on me didn't let up. I compromised with the colonel
and agreed to allow the restaurant to open if only 70% of the workers
had physicals, provided the remainder came in during the first week.
I did insist, however, that the manager's physical be done before opening. Once again, the colonel argued with me. He said the manager
wouldn't be handling food and therefore wouldn't need the certifi-
cate. I knew if this man were any kind of manager, he'd be in the
kitchen overseeing the food preparation and he needed the exam.
Then the colonel asked me if the manager could get his physical done
by his private physician in Saigon. I said no."

The angry colonel told Doug his obstinacy was hurting the
troops. He called Doug's commanding officer and demanded he do
something. Doug wouldn't budge. It was a standoff. Finally, the manager showed up for his physical. "I will never forget the phone call I
received from the lab tech who analyzed the manager's sputum specimen," said Doug. "He reported he had never seen so many tubercu-
lous organisms on one slide. They were fighting each other for space
under the microscope. The manager had such a horrible case of tuberculosis, it would have been a disaster if he had ever handled the
food."

• • • •

CHAPTER SEVENTEEN

• • • • • • • •

"The rats themselves used the traps for population control."

One afternoon, Doug called to ask if I would help him do tuberculosis skin testing on GIs who had shared a drinking cup with a Vietnamese worker diagnosed with TB. It was July, and the temperature was well over 110 degrees when we arrived at the unit. Doug asked the GIs to form two lines in front of us for the tests. Then he and I bent down to prepare the syringes. When we looked up, four soldiers stood on his line. The other thirty were on mine. To get through the dirt that was caked on each arm, I used three alcohol-soaked cotton balls. I tested all of the soldiers under the hot sun while Doug stood to the side, talking to the commander.

Tuberculosis was endemic to Vietnam. Graffiti in the bathroom on Wards 7 and 8 warned, "In Vietnam, all women either have TB or VD. If you want to screw someone, make sure she's coughing." At Valley Forge General Hospital, so many patients had TB that the bar they frequented just off base was nicknamed "The Sputum Cup."

In addition to tuberculosis, Doug monitored the rates of hepatitis and infectious diarrhea. "Strangely," he recalled, "I was not required to keep track of venereal disease, and I was rebuffed in my efforts to address what I knew was an escalating problem. The Korean army base just south of Long Binh allowed prostitutes to work on the base provided they show up for monthly VD checks. Since gonorrhea was becoming resistant to our usual antibiotics, I suggested to my commanding officer that we start monthly VD checks on prostitutes. Hundreds of them were working on or just off the base. He went into apoplexy. Apparently during World War II, when so many U.S. soldiers were drinking alcohol in the European towns, it was suggested that beer be made available to them by the military. Army public relations killed the idea. They worried that the American public would think the Army was turning clean-cut, gentlemanly soldiers into alcoholics. In Vietnam, the officials worried about doing anything that would be perceived as support of prostitution on an Army base, even though everyone knew it was going on. My CO told me to forget it. VD was not something I was supposed to be concerned with. No one took it seriously. Maybe they thought catching VD was part of being a true soldier." As prevalent, and apparently as acceptable, as VD was, when senior officers came to the 24th Evacuation Hospital with it, their medical records listed their ailment not as venereal disease, but as "non-specific urethritis."

Another one of Doug's jobs was to control the rat population on Long Binh Post. It was a difficult task because the post's considerable refuse attracted a lot of rats. "Vietnamese truckers, usually women, carried the garbage from the separate units on post to a square-mile sanitary landfill near the center of the base," explained Doug. "There, Vietnamese men and women, who made an art of scavenging, paid the U.S. government thousands of dollars to cull through it each evening. When a section was completely scavenged, fuel was poured over it and fires were set. Then dirt was plowed over the area, even as the fires smoldered. Organic refuse from the kitchens never made it to the landfill. Trucks transported it directly outside the gate for human and animal consumption."

Hospital waste was a real concern to Doug and his unit. At the 24th, we put it outside each ward where it was easy prey for rats unless it was picked up quickly. Corpsmen who took out the garbage at night found they had to scare the rats away to get the garbage into the can. Often, there weren't any cans, or no lids for the cans there were. One morning, Doug gave a hospital in-service on waste disposal. Usually after a lecture, we improved for a few days before we returned to sloppy habits, but Doug made sure his talk would not be forgotten. As he finished speaking, he reached into a large brown paper bag in front of him and pulled out a trap holding a live rat the size of a small dog. Twenty years later, he maintained only half in jest, "The rats themselves used the traps for population control. They pushed the most elderly among them into them to make room for the young."

Doug's unit did not have to trap the rats. That lucky job belonged to the 20th Preventive Medicine Unit. Though it was based at Long Binh, it did scientific sampling and culturing for the entire southern region of Vietnam. Techs from the 20th used *Have-a-Heart* traps to catch the rats alive because they wanted fleas to stay on the bodies. After catching a rat, they combed its fur and took a flea count. If the fleas exceeded a certain number, they placed the unit on alert for bubonic plague.

Rats were on all U.S. bases, in hooches and especially in bunkers (small fortified shelters). We heard of one inventive Green Beret sanitary engineer up north who tried to reduce the population by paying local villagers for each rat they brought to him. In time, he discovered his plan for eliminating the rats backfired. The villagers had begun to breed them for the bounty!

Along with the rats and their fleas, malaria-carrying mosquitoes were a concern. During monsoon season from May to December, units on Long Binh conducted an intensive campaign to eliminate potential breeding grounds for the insects. "Standing water was drained daily," said Doug. "If puddles couldn't be drained, insecticide was sprayed on them with hand-held foggers, the largest of which we called the 'mother-fogger.' On nights when the wind velocity was less than seven miles an hour, the entire base was sprayed from the air to catch mosquitoes in flight. The efforts were successful. Not a single case of malaria originated on post during 1971."

Long Binh's environment was not friendly to snakes either, but once Doug was called about a snake. It had been found at the WAC unit across the road from the 24th Evacuation Hospital. "Though my tropical medicine course at Walter Reed had not covered snakes," he remembered, "I grabbed some reference books and went to help the WACs. I found thirty women standing around a paper-thin corpse. So many rocks had been thrown at it and so many boots had stomped on it, I peeled it off the ground. It was almost transparent. Even if I had been trained to identify snakes, I couldn't have told anything about that one. In fact, I don't think the snake's mother would have known it."

• • • •

CHAPTER EIGHTEEN

• • • • • • • •

"Too bad he's married."

I first met Doug at the end of March, 1971. He had admitted a baby— the first of many— to Ward 7, and the little boy's scalp vein IV had come out. Though I had no problem putting an IV into any GI on the ward, I wanted no part of hurting an infant, so I called Doug to restart it. He arrived on Ward 7 within ten minutes, bounding through the rear door of the ward, dressed in a denim shirt and a pair of bell bottom slacks. I was astounded. In every way, he differed from the preventive medicine officer/pediatrician he had replaced. That doctor would have made any number of excuses not to come to the hospital before sulking his way through the door wearing week-old fatigues. Doug, happy to be caring for a baby, was more than willing to discuss the child's rare liver disease with me. He was animated, energetic and interesting. He was new to Vietnam.

In mid-April, I went with him on a med-cap to the Vietnamese hospital not far from the post. He joined me that evening for a "Cook Your Own Steak" party at the 24th Evac officers' club. We sat with some of the doctors and nurses from Wards 7 and 8, cooked our strip steaks on a fifty-gallon-drum grill, and danced to a Vietnamese band. Because of the Long Binh curfew, the party ended at ten. Doug and I talked in my room until four.

The following Sunday we drove to Saigon, a smog-ridden city, home to bars and bargirls, beggars and "cowboys" —teenagers on motorbikes who were able to cut the neckstrap of a camera and race off, camera in hand, without stopping. Narrow congested streets were filled with Vietnamese pedicabs and motorbikes, Army jeeps and trucks, French Citroens and old Pontiacs. Major intersections had sentry stations that stood on sandbags, surrounded by concertina wire. Doug and I paid attention to none of this. We started at the downtown market where vendors sold everything from underwear to live chickens. Then we skipped up the grassy parkway in the center of TuDo Street— one of the wide boulevards that gave Saigon its nickname, "Paris of the Orient" —and ran into a movie theater lobby just to smell the popcorn. We had lunch on a riverboat, visited the Saigon Zoo to see the few malnourished animals, and walked along tree-canopied streets in a residential area of the city. We stopped at a small community park that had swings and see-saws, though no children. Our day ended with dinner in the rooftop restaurant of the Caravelle Hotel, and because it was dark, even Saigon looked beautiful from the adjoining rooftop garden. Had the restaurant's picture windows not been taped to prevent shattering in case of a bomb blast and had we not been dressed in fatigues, we might have been in an elegant restaurant anywhere in the world. It was the most "normal" day I had had in five months.

Doug had been in-country for only a month when I met him. His enthusiasm duplicated my early excitement when I told my parents how much I enjoyed my work. He loved going on med-caps and was trying to discover as much as he could about Vietnam and its people. He even saw his preventive medicine responsibilities as a challenge, something new to master. I had been in-country for four months. I was bitter about the war and exhausted from the hard work. Doug's love of life, as well as his sincerity and caring brought out a part of me that I had long since forgotten. He got me through the year by restoring my ability to trust. In turn, when he became overwhelmed by the war, the waste, and the frustrations of his job, I helped him.

We had a great time together. If I worked the day shift, we ate dinner at one of the clubs on post or at the *Mandarin House*, or we partied with the staff from internal medicine. One night we went to a club on the far side of Long Binh to see *They Shoot Horses, Don't*

They? The projector had technical problems, and for two hours, we watched a vibrating, blurred image on the screen accompanied by inaudible dialogue. It never occurred to us to leave because it was the closest we had come to a first-run movie! Years later, I wondered if the "technical problem" was related to the fact that the movie starred Jane Fonda who was despised by soldiers for her support of the NVA.

Another night, Doug invited the four men who ran the *Mandarin House* to his hooch for an "All-American" barbeque. "They had always been so gracious to me," he said, "that I wanted to do something for them. My sergeant was able to get a fifteen-pound box of chicken, and we put together enough ingredients for a barbeque sauce and a salad. There was a rusty grill outside the hooch, but I don't know where we found charcoal, probably the PX. The Chinese men arrived with the *maitre d'* of the restaurant in tow and two young waiters carrying a roasted pig splayed on a platter with an apple in its mouth! A thick, even glaze coated the pig, and I'm sure some poor kitchen worker had been hand-turning it on a spit for the whole day. The *maitre d'* supervised the cutting of it into small squares of meat for each of us. The krackle, which was the roasted skin of the pig, was fantastic. The Chinese men explained that it was some kind of holiday for them that demanded they eat pig, but I didn't buy that for a minute. I think it was just another example of their generosity."

If I worked the night shift, Doug and I went on med-caps to the villages during the day. We made several weekend trips to Saigon in his lumbering International Harvester—precursor to today's sport utility vehicles. "When I first arrived in-country," he remembered, "I was disappointed that I had not been issued a jeep, but the first time I drove through monsoon rains that came at me horizontally, I was grateful I had sides and windows on the truck to protect me." On one trip to Saigon, we came out of a store to discover the Harvester had a flat tire. "We had no spare," said Doug, "and no way to get the tire fixed. Fortunately, there was a USO a few blocks away, and I planned to call the motor pool at Long Binh to find out what to do. While we waited for the phone, we struck up a conversation with an American civilian claiming to be in Saigon with the Agency for International Development (AID). He said he could get the tire fixed, so we went back to it. As we walked up, two young guys, about eighteen years old, pulled up on a 50cc Honda motorbike and offered to fix the flat. In Vietnamese, they negotiated with our new-found friend, took the wheel off the truck, and rode off with it. I was absolutely convinced we'd never see the tire again. The guy from AID assured me we would and took us to their makeshift 'service center' set up on a corner three blocks away. The two kids took the tire off the wheel and removed the inner tube from it. Then they placed a round patch they had cut from another inner tube on the hole. They put a piston on it and held it tight with a C-clamp. Then they filled the inside of the piston with gasoline and set it on fire. The heat sealed the patch to the inner tube in the time that it took for the gasoline to burn off. They put the tire on the wheel and rode back to my truck where they remounted it. The AID guy paid them and off they went. I kept that truck for at least another seven months and the tire never went flat."

On one weekend in June, Doug and I caught a military flight to Vung Tau to swim in the South China Sea, and toward the end of my tour, we went on "R&R" to Bangkok and Sydney.

Our relationship did not go unnoticed. One evening, a few weeks after we started going out, a lab tech who came to pick up specimens on Ward 7 surprised me by mentioning that I had been seen with the same man at several places on post. He wanted to know what was going on. My supervisor was even more blunt. Watching Doug leave the ward one morning, she turned to me and said, "He's such a nice guy. Too bad he's married." When I told her he was not, she fired back, "Oh, yes he is. The major checked his personnel records. She thinks you're spending too much time with him." The major was wrong on both counts.

Doug and I were fortunate. It was hard to sustain a healthy relationship in Vietnam because we were all emotionally disabled. To do our jobs, we nurses had to suppress our feelings or anesthetize them with alcohol. But at the same time, we needed connections to remind us we were human, to remind us we were women. "I just wanted someone to reach out to when I felt lower than a worm," one nurse told me.

The men had their own problems. Many of them believed that "all's fair in love and war," which made it difficult to figure out who was sincere and who was manipulative, who was honest and who

was lying, who was a real bachelor and who was a "geographical bachelor." I had been in-country for only a month when I wrote to a friend,
"The men I've met think all the rules have been suspended. They'll
say and do anything if it gets them what they want, not only with
women, but in every part of their lives." Until I met Doug, I trusted
no one.

Even healthy relationships were affected by the atmosphere
of suspended reality. Nothing about our lives was normal. There was
no rent to pay or car to get serviced. Food cost very little, and someone else did the laundry. We were able to put critical decisions on
hold for a year. We did not even have to file income tax returns until
we got back to the States. All we had to do was show up for work.

Every relationship was risky. If a nurse became involved with
an infantry soldier or a helicopter pilot, she did not know if one day
she would see him brought in on a dustoff. "I remember a nurse who
was engaged to a pilot," said John Miller. "One night, he was killed in
a flaming helicopter crash. She didn't know it until they brought his
burned body into the emergency room during her shift."

Many nurses became involved with married doctors. These
relationships grew out of friendships on the wards, where the bonds
were often the strongest. And when the separation came, the nurse
and doctor each returned to "the world" without the other's support,
unable to talk about or communicate with the one person who had
helped them through the year.

My head nurse, Judy Thoesen, came to Vietnam with her
husband, Rick. They had been married for less than a year when they
put in requests for overseas assignments. Rick, a sanitary engineer,
received orders for Vietnam, Judy's were for Okinawa. They tried to
change Rick's, but he was told his specialty was needed in Vietnam.
To stay with him, Judy volunteered for the war with no guarantee she
would be stationed near him. "When I arrived, the Chief Nurse at
USARV told me I was in Vietnam to serve, and I shouldn't worry
about being with my husband," remembered Judy. "I figured that comment spelled doom for us, so I didn't push it. But Rick convinced his
supervisor we should be together." When Judy was assigned to the
93rd Evacuation Hospital, Rick got orders for the 20th Preventive
Medicine Unit, also at Long Binh. "I was just happy to be with Rick,"

said Judy, "but unfortunately for him, his job was to be in charge of the motor pool— not quite what he was trained for."

Ironically, being married created problems for the couple at the 93rd Evac. "The commanding staff of the hospital was really resentful because their wives were at home and Rick had me there," Judy explained. "They were really paranoid. I don't know what the deal was. Lots of unmarried couples were staying together. But the CO placed a nightly guard at the nurses' quarters with specific orders to make sure married couples didn't stay together. It was all ass backwards."

When the hospital closed in April, 1971, Judy came to the 24th Evac and was assigned a room just inside the back door of hooch #4. Rick could come and go without bothering the nurses in the hooch. "Not that any of the other nurses cared," she recalled. Having Rick with her made Judy feel more secure. "The year didn't go any faster," she said. "It was still a long year. But I don't think I was as depressed as some of the people who were there on their own, the nurses who got involved with married doctors or married pilots. And I know Rick probably would have come home an alcoholic if I hadn't been there."

Because the nurses at the 24th Evacuation Hospital were so young, many had their first sexual experience in Vietnam. Often, it was not something they planned. A stateside physician had encouraged one nurse to carry birth control pills with her to Vietnam. "I'm not going to do that," she told him. "I won't need them." Fortunately for her, the hospital pharmacy stocked contraceptives.

If a nurse became pregnant, she had three alternatives. She could go home to process out of the Army—in 1971, military women were not allowed to have dependents. Her commanding officer and chief nurse decided when she got to leave Vietnam. The CO at the 24th Evac, a gynecologist, sent pregnant nurses home immediately. But I heard of a married nurse stationed up north whose chief nurse did not allow her to go home until her eighth month of pregnancy because she was angry with the nurse, who was pregnant when she arrived in Vietnam.

The second alternative was to go to Japan for an abortion under an assumed name. She, too, depended on the help of her hospital's commander or chief nurse. Frank Chamberlin said he unofficially facilitated trips for nurses and Red Cross women when he was commander in An Khe. "The Air Force had some flights for which the itineraries and departure times weren't publicized," he remembered. "I had to make a series of calls and get them to the right Air Force base at the right time for the flight to Japan. The women would come back and return to work in three days, or their stay in Vietnam would have been extended. It didn't happen often, thank goodness, but boys will be boys and girls will be girls. Boys and girls got together, and sometimes, the results were unwanted. I wasn't for or against abortion. It was their choice, not mine. I had to help them in any way I could."

Finally, a pregnant nurse could try to hide her pregnancy— not difficult in fatigues—and give birth in Vietnam. One staff nurse at the 24th Evac did this in mid-1970, much to the surprise of the commanding officer, an obstetrician who was called to the OR for the unexpected delivery. The nurse's husband was an Air Force pilot stationed on Guam, and she wanted to stay near him as long as possible. Everyone on the staff was thrilled by the birth.

• • • •

CHAPTER NINETEEN

• • • • • • • •

"You see, in the Army, women are second-class citizens."

The sound of scratching woke me up. Cursing under my breath, I rolled over expecting to see a small herd of Vietnamese cockroaches scrambling up the wall of my room. Instead, I found myself looking directly into the face of a man framed in my window. To improve his view, he had climbed on the decaying sandbags that surrounded the hooch, dislodging sand and creating the noise that awakened me. I leaped out of bed shouting, "Shush, shush, get away!!" frantically waving my arms at him as though he were a cat. Startled, he jumped off his perch. I turned to my door, intending to use the phone in the hall to call for help and realized my room was the one closest to the hooch's unlocked entrance. I listened for movement in the hall. After fifteen minutes and no sound, I slowly unlocked my door and opened it. The hall was empty.

It was not the "Peeping Tom's" first appearance at the nurses' quarters, nor would it be his last. Hospital administrators, aware of him for several weeks, did nothing to apprehend him. The chief nurse told us to put opaque curtains on the windows, even suggesting we use terrycloth towels. A week after I saw him, he broke into the room of a nurse who lived in hooch #4. At her screams, several men came to her aid from other rooms in the hooch. They caught the intruder and the nurse was sent to a hospital elsewhere in-country to be with her fiancé. Presumably, the problem was over.

In fact, our problems had just begun. The executive officer, appalled that so many men had been spending the night in nurses' rooms, announced at a staff meeting that he wanted to "crack down on the loose morals of the nurses." He threatened to have a ten-foot high chain-link fence erected around our quarters. Word spread among the nurses that it was an idle threat because chain-link fencing was not readily available in Vietnam. However, forty-eight hours later and over our heated objections, he fenced us in under a double standard that dictated military men could have liaisons whenever and wherever they wanted, but military women, particularly nurses, could not.

In his haste to throw the chain-link chastity belt around us, the executive officer forgot that the officers' club was in the midst of the nurses' quarters. He had penned in the foxes with the chickens! To meet the challenge, he requested troops from the MP unit on post to stand guard at our quarters, armed with a sign-in book and M-16s. They turned him down. Then he assigned corpsmen, the ones with whom we worked, to guard us. It was as frustrating for them as it was for us, because they already put in twelve-hour workdays and they wanted to relax when they were off duty. In a letter to my parents I wrote, "I haven't been so upset about anything these lifers and guardians of the public welfare have come up with. Nothing like caging in women who are at least twenty-one years of age, have lived independently, made life-and-death decisions, and slave seventy-two hours a week in their hospital." Using a popular phrase of the era, I finished with, "I believe there's a credibility gap here." My parents never responded to my rage, but I can bet they were less upset than I about the fence and the guards. As it turned out, on most nights we brought snacks to the corpsmen and visited with them while they guarded our morals.

As women in Vietnam, we faced a variety of problems related to our gender that were intrinsic to the military. When boot camp instructors call soldiers "girls" or "ladies" to insult them, it is impossible for the same soldiers and their officers to regard women as anything but inferior. In "this man's army" of 1971, women had a limited role, and the men believed it was their right to determine what that role should be. At best, this led to uncomfortable situations

for us, and at worst, it contributed to outright harassment and attacks. While our patients had nothing but respect for us, many officers, particularly the rear echelon types at Long Binh, believed that
women were in the army to meet their needs—enlisted women their
clerical and sexual needs, nurses their need to be nurtured. Unless of
course a man decided a nurse should meet his sexual needs. Then it
became open season on us. "The nurses I worked with were being hit
on constantly," said Chris Slavsky. "I felt bad for them, but I guess it
was human nature. The enlisted guys didn't even try. It had been
drummed into our heads that we weren't officers and didn't have the
rights of an officer."

Twenty-one years after I left Vietnam, I shared the chain-
link fence story with a group of women veterans attending a dinner
in Washington, DC, and told them how angry I was that the major
thought he could decide for us what was morally right. Across the
table from me, a nurse spoke up, "If you think that was bad," she said,
"I have a story to top yours!"

Wendy Wall, the daughter of a career military officer, had
her flight to Vietnam delayed enroute several times by the February,
1969, post-Tet counteroffensive. When the plane finally circled Bien
Hoa Airbase to land, she and her fellow passengers looked down to
see soldiers in hand-to-hand combat on the landing strip below them.
The pilot quickly pulled up and landed at Cam Ranh Bay, hundreds
of miles up the coast. Wendy and the four other nurses were told they
had to get themselves to USARV Headquarters. Despite intense fighting all over the country, the five women hopped a series of Army and
Air Force planes and made it safely to Long Binh without the assistance of any military authority. They were put up in the nurses' quarters at the 93rd Evacuation Hospital.

"That night," recalled Wendy, "the hospital came under fire.
There was fighting in the compound. We were told to lie on the floor
of the hooches in flak jackets and helmets. I heard people running
and shouting. Then I heard small-arms fire. Flares lit up the entire
area." When it was over and the nurses were allowed to stand up, she
thanked the young soldier, armed with an M-16, who stood at the
entrance to the quarters. "Thank you very much for guarding us," she
said. "I really felt safe with you here." Wendy remembered he had a

"funny look" on his face as she spoke, and when she finished, he said, "Well ma'am, I wasn't here to protect you. Actually, we were supposed to shoot the nurses if we got overrun." Wendy thought it was a joke.

The next morning at breakfast, she told the regular staff members what he had said and mentioned that she thought his humor was a strange way of coping. "Instead of smiling," said Wendy, "they assured me he wasn't kidding. They said they had been told that if the hospital were overrun, they wouldn't be captured. The five of us who were new looked at each other as if to say, 'This isn't for real.' It was quite a shock. I thought in Vietnam if it was necessary to defend themselves, women would get weapons, like in the wild West days. I refuse to believe an American private, who couldn't have been more than eighteen years old, would be able to turn his M-16 on the nurses. Maybe that's my coping mechanism. If it was a true policy, I wonder how he dealt with it."

The surprise was not only that the women had not been armed—in an environment where eighteen-year-old "men" were armed to the hilt— but that it had been assumed that they would prefer to be shot rather than be captured. No one, of course, had checked with the women.

Months later, while she was stationed at the 95th Evac Hospital at Da Nang, Wendy was equally surprised when the hospital's executive officer (XO) briefly considered arming the staff nurses, this time to protect them from American soldiers. "We were concerned about a Peeping Tom," explained Wendy. "He had a high-powered telescope and frequently called us on the phone in our quarters to tell us exactly what we were doing. The XO said he would look into supplying us with .45s. They never came through, but some nurses bought .38s on the black market to protect themselves." She then added sarcastically, "Isn't it wonderful that we couldn't get weapons to defend ourselves from the enemy, but they'd consider it for protection against Americans."

Not all the peeping was done from a distance. Wendy remembered one night when she left the officers' club to return to her room. "I started to get undressed," she said, "and I felt like someone was watching me. Under the bed, I found one of the officers who had left the club ahead of me." Men harassed the nurses in other ways at the 95th. "One soldier stood outside our screen doors always talking about sex," Wendy recalled, "and another guy put his hand through the screen to open a door latch. The nurse in the room hit his hand with a hammer. No one got a look at him, but the day after, we kept an eye out for someone with an injured hand."

We women were responsible for extricating ourselves from "difficult situations." If we did not want a soldier looking in our windows, we had to cover them. If we were bothered by aggressive senior officers, it was up to us to fend them off, preferably without offending them. Wendy remarked, "I don't think anything was ever done to anyone who bothered us. There was a sense that if we were in the Army in a war zone, we'd have to put up with the good ol' boy games."

The word "sexual harassment" was not yet part of our vocabulary. In fact, the language of the women's movement was so rudimentary that the only term we knew was "male chauvinist pig" (or "mcp"). I used it one day when I took a call from a captain inviting nurses to a unit party on Long Binh. I agreed to post the time and place for the party on the hooch bulletin board, but that was not enough for him. He said he would like the group, preferably at least ten, to include blondes, brunettes and redheads between 5'4" and 5'7," no one too heavy, and all interested in having fun. I felt like a clerk at the supply depot! The captain saw nothing unusual in his request and was surprised when I called him an "mcp," a term he had not yet encountered. I filed the party information in the trash.

Many experiences made us uncomfortable. At the PX we could not get near the magazine rack because of the crowds of GIs standing in front of it looking at *Penthouse* and *Playboy*. In the larger officers' clubs like the USARV club, though it did not happen often, we had to be prepared for female singers to finish the show with a striptease. Many of us were subjected to verbal harassment or touching, and some of us were assaulted and raped. Most incidents were not reported, and the reported ones were not taken seriously because they were accepted as an integral part of a military at war. In the mid-'80s, a survey was done of 257 nurses who served in Vietnam. More than 50% of the respondents reported they had been sexually harassed, most often by sexual remarks, physical contact such as touching, and requests for sex.[26] The harassment we faced happens to women all the time. But it was particularly galling in Vietnam because we faced it during a war in which we and the men were supposed to be on the same side with the same mission.

Unofficial practices thwarted us. There was no regulation prohibiting women from having a military driver's license, but it "just wasn't done." Before 1971, individual women had challenged the custom and obtained licenses, yet it remained a well-entrenched practice when Stephanie Genthon Kilpatrick took it on.

"Ward 2 was organizing a party," she recalled, "and we needed to go somewhere to pick up something. Nobody available to go had a license. When we couldn't have a party because of the mess-up, I was determined it wouldn't happen again. I went to the motor pool on post to apply for a license. The clerk told me, 'We don't give them to women.' I asked to see the regulation that said women couldn't have a license. 'It's not a regulation,' he said. 'We just don't do it.' Then the captain, who must have been listening from the back room, came in and said, 'It's all right, let her go ahead and take the test. She won't pass anyway.' I got a booklet to study. A week later I passed the written test. Then the captain said to the clerk, 'Don't worry. She can't drive a truck.' At that point, I said to myself, 'Come hell or high water, I *will* drive this truck!'" Stephanie, 5'4" tall, climbed into the cab of a two-and-a-half ton truck and drove away. "The guys were stunned," she said, and added proudly, "We never missed any more parties."

In addition to the harassment and informal discrimination, we faced biased official policies. A nurse who worked with me in internal medicine was responsible for the dismantling of two of them. Ann's husband was a university student in Iowa. Because he did not have a dependent's ID card, he was barred from using the PX and commissary at a local base while she was in Vietnam. The wife of a male soldier automatically received a military dependent's ID card, but the husband of a servicewoman had to document that his wife provided more than half of his income to qualify for an ID. A second bias related to separation pay—a bonus paid to compensate men for being away from their spouses. It was automatically awarded to married men stationed overseas, but married women, including Ann, were ineligible for it.

Angry about the blatant inequity of the regulations, Ann went to the Long Binh personnel office to apply for an ID card for her husband and separation pay for herself. "Sorry, ma'am," said the desk sergeant, "I can't let you apply for them." He broke into a broad smile as he continued, "You see, in the Army, women are second-class citizens." Ann immediately wrote to her senator, Harold Hughes. He insisted that official policy could not be discriminatory and assured her that his staff would find the appropriate regulation to obtain what she deserved. A month later, he sent her an apology and included with his letter a copy of the bill he had introduced in Congress to correct the inequity. The bill's preface quoted the smiling desk sergeant.

• • • •

CHAPTER TWENTY

• • • • • • • •

"Serving you from the Delta to the DMZ."

As Christmas, 1970, approached, Wards 7 and 8 won the 24th Evac's ward decorating contest. Our theme, "Home for the Holidays," came from a desire to create a holiday oasis for the soldiers. We put red brick paper and tinsel around the nurses' stations and hung stockings all over the wards, tagged with the names of nurses, doctors, corpsmen and patients. With construction paper, we turned the entrance to each of the wards into a welcoming Dutch door, complete with snow-covered windows. On the door to Ward 8, we wrote "Welcome!" Ward 7's door wished everyone "Love." Small Santa's hats decorated our two Christmas trees. On Christmas morning, we wore those hats when we awakened the patients, and we would have kept them on all day had the supervisor not reprimanded us for being out of uniform. Winning the decorating contest was a real bonus for us because the prize was a large SONY radio. After that, the internal medicine unit had music from the time the station went on the air at 6:00 AM until it signed off at midnight!

AFVN (Armed Forces Vietnam Network), "serving you from the Delta to the DMZ," was based in Saigon and had both AM and FM stations as well as a television station. On the AM dial, we heard a variety of rock and country-and-western sounds. For the entire year I was in Vietnam, the most-often-played song on the radio was *I Beg Your Pardon, I Never Promised You a Rose Garden* (as if we needed reminding). In the clubs, the song most often played by the live rock groups was *We Gotta Get Out of this Place* (never played on the radio). AFVN-FM carried "easy listening music," which meant elevator music. The DJs on AFVN were enlisted men and women from all branches of the military.

Eighteen years after I left Vietnam, one of those DJs provided insight for me into the military radio network. Betty Anne Addy Horning had been a twenty-one-year-old Marine sergeant with Armed Forces Radio and TV in 1967. Though she was "the weather girl" for the 6:00PM and 11:00PM news in Okinawa, her shows were broadcast in Vietnam. Keeping the listening audience's attention for the weather report was a challenge for Betty Anne. "It was always the same," she remembered. "It was the rainy season or not the rainy season. That was the only change. After three days, I was tired of it, so I'd pick different states, take information from the AP tickertape, and tell the guys what the weather was like back home." She also wrote the news reports with adjusted casualty figures. "We'd get figures for the NVA and the VC that we had killed," she explained, "and deliberately double or triple them. If we felt statistics on Americans were too high, we'd cut them, especially if it was around a holiday. I was a Marine. We had always been told we were good for three or five of the enemy. I swear, if you added up all the numbers of dead and wounded enemy reported during the war, it would come out to three or four times the actual number. After I had changed the numbers for the newsman, he'd change them when he read them. It was almost as if the figures came out of thin air."

In time, Betty Anne was given her own nightly show which she called *The Girl Next Door*. Much to her dismay, programming for her show was pre-arranged. She wanted to play the Beatles, Beach Boys and Motown, but found herself restricted to Johnny Ray and Frank Sinatra. At the same time, the Okinawan radio station was playing '60's American rock music, even though its DJs did not speak English. One night, Betty Anne taped Aretha Franklin's *Respect* from the native station and played it repeatedly on armed forces radio. "I had to cut off the beginning and the end of it because of the Okinawan announcer's talking," she remembered, "but I played enough of the song for it to become a hit among the troops. After that, I was able to start playing some decent music."

In addition to music, AFVN offered advice pertinent to our daily lives. Regular announcements reminded us to "wash our feet once a day, change our socks daily and rotate our boots regularly." Frequent spots advised us to keep our M-16s clean. And each Monday, when DJs instructed us to take our malaria pills, GIs all over the country lined up for the big orange pill. At the 24th, bowls filled with the pills were at the entrance to the mess hall.

We had a TV on each ward in the hospital, and AFVN-TV carried the Super Bowl, World Series, and other important sports events—most in the middle of the night because of the time difference—as well as reruns of *Gunsmoke, Bonanza,* and *The Ed Sullivan Show.* The patients loved *Laugh-In* and *The Flip Wilson Show.* There were no commercials on TV, but the extra minutes were filled with Army plugs and character guidance from celebrities like Yankee great, Joe DiMaggio, who reminded us it was not a good thing to smoke marijuana.

Radio and TV filled the days and evenings for patients and staff. Unless a special event was aired, the stations signed off at midnight with the national anthems of South Vietnam and the United States. Listening to them, we joked that the Star-Spangled Banner would never again sound quite right to us without the accompanying Vietnamese national anthem.

• • • •

CHAPTER TWENTY-ONE

* * * * * * * *

"I haven't had a bath in a year!"

We nurses turned each of our rooms into a personal oasis. To keep the war at bay, we ordered curtains and bedspreads from the Sears catalog, closed our doors, turned on soft music and lowered our lights. Stephanie Genthon's room was the best one in hooch #3. It was paneled in knotty pine and had a built-in bed, bookcases, drawers and a closet. At an informal auction in late 1970, Stephanie, the highest bidder, had paid its previous occupant fifty dollars for the room. When she left Vietnam six months later, she passed it to me free-of-charge. One night, soon after I moved in, I questioned the gift she had given me.

My lights were off and I was drifting into sleep when something fell onto my pillow. In a single motion, I bolted from the bed and turned on the light to see a giant cockroach wiggling on its back, two inches from where my head had been. I looked up to find six of his fat friends watching me from their perch at the top of the wood paneling.

I was no stranger to cockroaches. In fact, I had co-habited with hundreds of them in my New York City apartment. But these were unlike New York cockroaches. Vietnamese cockroaches resembled two-inch, armored and winged cigar-butts. When you stepped on them in combat boots, they splattered with a crunch in a circle four inches in diameter. Sometimes, if your boot hit them at just the right angle, you would slide through their mushy interiors as though you had stepped on a banana peel.

When I first arrived in-country, I was warned to check the inside of my boots every morning for cockroaches and lizards before putting them on. I did not mind doing that. Nor did it upset me whenever I found three or four of the giant roaches on an unwashed plate I left out after dinner or a snack. But I drew the line at having to share my pillow with them.

I turned to Doug for help. As the Preventive Medicine Officer of Long Binh Post, he had access to the pesticide Diazinon. After he sprayed behind the knotty pine panels, I had no more problem. But in the process of being eliminated, the tenacious cockroaches gave Doug a run for his money. One evening, he chased a group of three, only to have them turn in a counterattack. When they came at him, his 6'2" body cleared the floor by a foot!

A few weeks later, I had another encounter with Vietnamese wildlife in my room when I opened the door, flipped on the light, and saw a rat jump out of my closet. Without missing a step or making a sound, I carefully reached for a bottle of *Chivas Regal* scotch from my bookcase shelf and grabbed an empty orange crate from the hall. Leaning against the wall across from my room, I sat on the crate and sipped scotch from the bottle while I watched the two-inch opening under my door. I do not know how long I was there nor how much scotch I drank, but in time, the rat came out and ran down the hall away from me. I went into my room, put a towel across the base of my door, and went to sleep.

Doug not only rid my room of giant cockroaches, he improved the quality of life for all the nurses at the 24th Evac. The hospital's chief nurse asked him, as the Preventive Medicine Officer, to investigate the high rate of absenteeism among staff nurses. "I cross-referenced complaints with a list of where the nurses lived and worked," explained Doug, "and I soon realized there was no common pattern to the absenteeism. So I scheduled interviews with twenty-five nurses who had been sick. Halfway through the interviews, it became obvious I was dealing with a real morale problem. The nurses complained of exhaustion and overwork. They were angry that the elective surgery being done by the surgeons, like rounding out the eyes of Vietnamese women, kept them working extended hours. Their hours were totally out of keeping with what everyone else on the hospital staff was doing."

Doug convinced the chief nurse to give us an extra half-day off each week. Shortening our week from six days to five-and-a-half gave us a chance to wind down from work and still enjoy a full day off. The chief nurse also agreed to let us take short breaks during our twelve-hour shifts. Finally, she and the hospital commander gave us permission to catch helicopter flights to Vung Tau on our days off. Within weeks of instituting the changes, the absenteeism rate dropped markedly.

But Doug was not finished. "While I was interviewing the nurses," he said, "I was amazed at the number of women who told me if I really wanted to be of value, I should do something about the vaginitis that was plaguing them. It seemed to be epidemic. I discovered that the hoochmaids were washing their clothes, including their underwear, on the floor of the shower stalls. There was so much algae growing on the shower floors that the nurses wore flip-flops when they showered, and here, their undergarments were being washed in the stuff. Added to that were the very long hours they worked, the lack of breaks to change their clothes, their sweatiness, and the lack of a bathtub. It was no wonder they had problems."

Doug found a washer and a dryer in a storeroom on post and had it installed in one of the hooches so we could wash our own underwear. Unfortunately, he could not locate a bathtub for us.

For that, we had to wait for "R & R." More than any single aspect of life in "the world," we missed a hot bath. So when Stephanie and I went to Hong Kong in May, we each packed several jars of bath oil beads and crystals, dreaming of what lay ahead. After we checked into the luxurious Hong Kong Hotel, the bellman showed us to our room on the eighteenth floor. He barely had a chance to open the door before we pushed the poor man aside in a race to the bathroom. Stephanie arrived first and joyfully cried out in her rich Mississippi drawl, "Ma-a-ry, they have a bathtub!!" The bellman, trying to be helpful, enthusiastically agreed and added, "We have a shower, too." "Oh, that doesn't count," answered Stephanie. "I haven't had a bath in a year." The courteous bellman walked to the door without comment.

. . . .

CHAPTER TWENTY-TWO

• • • • • • • •

"Mary has changed..."

On her way out of Vietnam, Stephanie was rocketed at the 90th Replacement Battalion. "Four hours from getting on the plane," she remembered, "shells were falling and I was in a bunker." She landed in San Francisco, and her luggage was stolen at the airport when a bus driver insisted on pulling away from it at a curb. She sat in uniform at the Dallas airport for fourteen hours, and no one spoke to her. "By the time I got to Mississippi," she said, "I had spent four days on the road in the same clothes, and no one, military or civilian, had said 'Welcome Home' or even 'How are you?' Being ignored by military people was harder for me than being ignored by civilians."

She did not realize she was angry. "I just knew I was miserable," she explained. "I stayed miserable for years. I never vented my anger. I wouldn't trust myself. There was so much I couldn't tell. My parents were so proud I went, so proud I was there, so proud when I came home. They never knew that I didn't want to go. They never knew that I hated it."

When Stephanie went to Vietnam, she did not think of herself as a good nurse. When she came back, she thought, "Damn, I'm good. I can apply for any job and do it." She soon realized that "No one was interested in a nurse whose expertise was taking care of patients blown up by claymore mines and booby traps." In fact, no one cared what she or any other nurse had done in Vietnam. The war, however, had left its mark on her. She said, "I remember thinking the

greatest thing that was going to happen to me professionally was that
I was no longer going to have to take care of a person who died for no
good reason. I went to work in the open-heart recovery room at Emory
in Atlanta. The first patient who died was a three-year-old little girl. I
lost it. I totally lost it. The mother and I were both in there, hugging
the baby. They finally took me to the emergency room to be examined. I had spent a whole year thinking when I got home it was going
to be so wonderful. It wasn't."

• • • •

My tour nearing its end, I checked into the 90th Replacement Battalion, gave my urine specimen for drug testing, and moved
into the women's quarters I had occupied a year before. I took the
room furthest from the slamming screen door and selected a cot with
a mosquito net. This time, I was not going to stay awake scratching!
But sleep came no more easily than it had on my first night in-country. I was afraid to go home— happy to be leaving Vietnam, but afraid
to go home. For an entire year, I had given little thought to what lay
beyond my DEROS, but I was certain I would not fit into the space I
had left in "the world."

Ironically, I had to miss the first flight out of Bien Hoa for
which I was scheduled. The previous February, I had become a captain by extending my enlistment for ninety days to give me the required one year left in grade. It took a lot for me to sign the extension,
but I did so after making some calculations. I knew that if I arrived at
the Oakland Army Terminal with fewer than ninety days left in the
Army, the time would be dropped, and I would be discharged. Ninety
or more days would send me to a new assignment. At the 90th, when
I was offered a seat on the earlier flight, — the one Terry Corneil
took— I realized that crossing the International Date Line would have
put me in California too early.

So I waited for the next "freedom bird." As on the trip over,
I was one of a handful of women on the flight. This time I sat in an
aisle seat near the front of the plane. Cheers erupted in the cabin
when we took off at 1:00AM on November 16th, when we left Vietnam airspace, and when we landed at Travis Air Force Base at 6:00AM
on the 15th. Suddenly, with no fanfare, the year was over. Those of us

who were processing out of the Army took a bus to the Oakland Army Terminal. Eight hours after arriving in California, I was a civilian.

We were met by silence, not angry crowds. By late 1971, indifference had replaced anti-war sentiment in the U.S. Even at Travis, the baggage handlers said nothing to us as we collected our suitcases in the early morning light, and at the Army Terminal, no one welcomed us home during the hours we spent going office to office to fill out the proper discharge forms. My last stop was at the airline ticket desk, where, to the surprise of the sergeant on duty, I insisted on paying a higher fare and flying to New York in civilian clothes. I was not afraid of being attacked by anti-war protesters. My Class A Army uniform (the office suit, not the fatigues) was the most tangible symbol of the wrong I had seen in the previous year, and I wanted to separate myself from it as soon as possible.

My parents were thrilled I was home, and so were my friends. Most everyone I met asked what it was *really* like, but they all seemed to want a brief answer. No one wanted to hear that a war was going on and that soldiers were still being wasted. After the first few days, the questions stopped, perhaps because the answers were not forthcoming. I had no words for anyone who had not been to Vietnam — they could not understand.

Like Stephanie, anger was my only emotion, and it stayed suppressed most of the time. However, one night my father became the target of my year's rage when he praised Richard Nixon for "bringing the boys home." More than my mother, he represented the blind patriotism that had refused to question our government's actions, had willingly sent GIs into the jungle and kept them there long after they should have been withdrawn. He let me vent for half an hour without responding, but a few days later I heard him say to a friend, "Mary has changed…"

At first I was disoriented. Had it not been for letters from Doug and the snapshots I brought home, I would have wondered if I had really been in Vietnam. Nor did I feel part of the world to which I had returned. Not long after I got home, I went with my mother to my brother's hockey game. When a fight broke out on the ice, the fans rose to their feet to cheer the participants, to applaud the violence. I sat in the stands next to my mom, tears quietly streaming down my cheeks, knowing full well that all violence is the same.

I could not look at an American flag with pride. Then, in August, 1974, Richard Nixon resigned. I was in graduate school at the University of Colorado at Denver and had just completed a final exam in statistics when I heard his resignation speech. On the way home, I passed a bank where an employee was lowering the flag in the setting Colorado sun. Nixon was gone, the law had won. For the first time in three years, I proudly watched the stars and stripes come down a pole.

After a shaky adjustment of our relationship to the demands of the world— the ones we avoided in Vietnam— Doug and I were married in 1973. Our experiences in Vietnam worked their way to the recesses of our minds to be called forward only by a particularly beautiful sunset, the aromas of Asian restaurants, or a visit to Chris and Carolyn Slavsky. Even then, our "Vietnam conversations" were short and filled with very specific factual memories, never feelings. Anger was the only feeling we allowed ourselves, and without realizing it, we stayed away from conversations that would trigger it. Unlike the rest of America, we saw no humor in *M*A*S*H*.

The fall of Saigon to the North Vietnamese in April, 1975, marked a turning point for the two of us, but we did not realize it when it happened. Sadness overwhelmed us as we watched the TV footage of Hueys being pushed off ships into the South China Sea and refugees clinging to the skids of helicopters on the roof of the U.S. Embassy. We grieved for the waste of life (American and Vietnamese) and the uselessness of the war and felt that as a nation, we should be keening. But we were relieved that the U.S. was finally out of Vietnam. We hoped that the Vietnamese people, without our war, would finally be able to move forward. Looking back on it, Doug and I now understand that the fall of Saigon made the Vietnam War safe for us to discuss because it had been pushed into the past tense, it had become history. Not long after, we even began to watch *M*A*S*H*.

But my feelings remained fairly undefined until early 1990 when I attended the three-day retrospective in Binghamton and heard that arrogant colonel's alibis about the war. Only when I connected with the veteran did I understand the pain beneath my anger. And only when I heard the colonel speak, did I remember the lie that caused my pain.

• • • •

EPILOGUE

. . . .

"We were wrong, terribly wrong," wrote Robert McNamara.[27] I knew we were wrong when we healed GIs, only to send them back to the bush and hope they would make it out of Vietnam alive. Stephanie knew we were wrong when she zipped kids into bodybags and tried to remember names. Chris knew we were wrong when he patched up self-inflicted wounds. John knew we were wrong when he evacuated Cambodian families who were victims of "friendly" fire. Terry knew we were wrong when he compared the air-conditioned hooches and stocked bars of the rear to the poncho liners and mosquito nets of the bush. Frank knew we were wrong when military leaders closed their eyes to the drug problem. Doug knew we were wrong when he cared for children with almond-shaped eyes and curly red hair. Son knew we were wrong when we refused to rebuild the country we destroyed. We all knew we were wrong when we watched the war become an industry that had a bottom line more concerned with loss of profits than loss of lives. In Vietnam, America lost the best of herself, and with it went a part of each of us.

Robert McNamara acknowledged mistakes. But he did it twenty-eight years too late and without the emotion one would expect from a man whose silence led to the deaths of millions. He was not the sole architect of the Vietnam War. Others went to their graves without confessing their ignorance of Vietnamese culture, their refusal to listen to experts, and their deception of the American public. Richard Nixon may have left office a defeated man, but he was never held liable for the appalling loss of life caused by his need to achieve a victory on paper. He was buried as a hero, ironically, as a man who brought East and West together.

Military leaders, defended by the colonel at SUNY Binghamton, complain that no one listened to them, that their hands were tied, that no declaration of war was behind them, that Washington gave them no mission, no direction and no leadership. But military commanders saw what I saw: that Vietnam was a primitive country, peopled by villagers concerned not with an abstract ideology but with the source of their next meal, that our presence was destroying the people we had come to save, that the government we backed was corrupt, and that poor leadership was wasting GIs. Yet it did not stop them from falling in line with the civilians they despised and sending hundreds of thousands of American kids into the jungle. Career officers and NCOs, disheartened by the character of the war and the ethical disintegration of the armed forces, quietly resigned from the Army. Young infantry soldiers, the grunts, had no voice and no escape.

Americans have never taken responsibility for what we did in Vietnam. We claim the war was fought in our living rooms, but the conflict raged for years before dissent became mainstream. Even then, opposition was related not to the morality of the war, but to the elusiveness of victory. We expected to win. Failing that, we wanted to cut our losses and bail out rather than examine what we had done to the people of Southeast Asia. By 1968, the Vietnam War dropped to seventh place on the Associated Press' Top Ten Stories of the year.[28] While we lost interest, the GIs fought the war's bloodiest battles.

Eighteen and nineteen-year-old kids carried the burden of the war we asked them to fight. They carried it in the jungle, they carried it when they were spat upon, they carried it when they could not get jobs. They carry it today in their destroyed bodies, in their nightmares, and in their genes altered by Agent Orange. They did what we asked them to do, and we turned from them.

As a nation, it is time for us to take the burden from the kids who fought our war. All of us were part of the lie that wasted an

American generation and devastated an ancient culture half a world away. Until we acknowledge the wrong that we did in arrogance, we will not have learned. And if we have not learned, we will do it again.

• • • •

WHERE WE ARE TODAY

• • • • • • • •

Stephanie Genthon Kilpatrick lives with her husband, Dick, in Brookhaven, Mississippi. After leaving Vietnam, she worked as a staff nurse in an open heart recovery room as well as in a kidney dialysis unit. She was the Director of Nursing at a community hospital but left that position when she felt she did not have an adequate impact on patient care. Today, she is a manager for workers' compensation cases and she reviews insurance claims. She has remained in the U.S. Army Reserves.

John Miller served as a U.S. Navy pilot for six years before securing a conscientious objector discharge from the Navy and founding a peace organization, *Peace Engineering, Inc.* He has continued to fly, first with an airline freight company and then with Pan American Airlines. He currently flies for another small freight airline. He lives just outside of Orlando, Florida.

Frank Chamberlin completed a Master's Degree in Health Administration at Baylor University when he returned from Vietnam. He eventually retired from the Army as a colonel after twenty-one years of service and began a private medical practice in Quincy, Illinois. When the hours became too demanding, Frank took a position as Medical Director of the Illinois Veterans Home. In December, 1992, he succumbed to cancer after a two-year struggle. He is buried at Arlington National Cemetery.

Son Dinh Nguyen and his wife, Kim, live in San Jose, California. They both work in Silicon Valley. He repairs computers, she is an electronics inspector. Their daughter, Kathie, graduated with a degree in business from San Jose State College.

Chris Slavsky returned to Colorado when he was discharged from the Army. He would have liked to have stayed in the health care field, but none of his work in Vietnam would have counted toward the requirements for a nursing license. Chris became a carpenter. He has worked in construction and has owned several small businesses. He currently works for a floor finishing company. Chris, his wife Carolyn, and their family live north of Colorado Springs in the foothills of the Rocky Mountains.

Terry Corneil made the Army his career for twenty-two years, including several tours in Europe, working in combat development and inspecting Russian missile facilities under the terms of the Intermediate-range Nuclear Forces (INF) Treaty. He left the service to join a not-for-profit environmental foundation as the Director of International Programs. Today, he is vice president of an environmental fuels company that produces clean fuels, estimated to reduce nitrogen oxides and particulates emitted from engines, turbines, and boilers by up to 80%. He and his wife, Mary Neal, live in Reno, Nevada.

Doug Powell completed his final year of pediatric training at the University of Colorado. After three years of general pediatric practice, he completed a fellowship in neonatology (care of critically ill newborns). He has been a neonatologist for twenty-two years in Colorado, Michigan, New York and Ohio. He has never grown tired of caring for the littlest people.

Mary Reynolds Powell has worked in community health and on community issues since her return from Vietnam. She received a Master's Degree in Urban Sociology from the University of Colorado. She and Doug have raised three wonderful children, and today they live in Shaker Heights, Ohio.

ACKNOWLEDGEMENTS

• • • • • • • •

If anyone had told me in Vietnam that one day people would be interested in hearing our story, much less that I would write it, like Frank Chamberlin, I would have said they were "f—ing crazy." But the story has been written and it has not been a solitary effort. At each stage of a process so new to me, someone has challenged me to take the steps that led to the work before you. Through their interest, concern and encouragement, each one raised the bar for me. I am indebted to them and to all my friends who kept asking, "How's the book?"

To Masha Britten, favorite instructor at Columbia, who invited me to speak at SUNY Binghamton. She would not take "no" for an answer, responding, "It's you we want." To Donna Taccini, who, after reviewing my first draft said, "We have a problem," and walked me to the next phase. To Liz Fowler, Barbara Finkelstein, Larry Cohen, and especially, Kathy Ewing, for their patient editing. To Susan Shipley, Shelly Schneeweis and Barbara Hesselman Kautz, all with me at the 24th Evac, for their efforts to make sure I got it right. To Jessica Powell and Mark Hoffman for their graphic assistance, and Cathy Powell for her input. To Jim Banks and Claudia Boatright, for their testimonials, but even more, for the many invitations to speak that provided the energizing feedback I needed to keep going. To Ned Grossman for his advice, David Hackworth, for his foreword, John Wilson, for his testimonial and Jim Boyd, for his inspiration. To Clint Greenleaf, for his enthusiasm and Betty Chamberlin, for her encouragement. To my wonderful family, particularly Doug, for their unfailing support of this effort. To all those whose voices are in this book. You shared your hearts with me. I hope I have done you justice.

A World of Hurt:
Between Innocence and Arrogance in Vietnam

Reference Notes

1. Stephanie Genthon Kilpatrick (1991) conversation with author, Brookhaven, MS

2. Perry, Mark. (1969) *Four Stars: the Inside Story of the Forty-year Battle between the Joint Chiefs of Staff and America's Civilian Leaders.* Boston: Houghton Mifflin. p. 159

3. Summers, Harry. (1982) *On Strategy: a Critical Analysis of the Vietnam War.* Novata: Presidio. p. 96

4. ibid. p. 96

5. Perry p. 163

6. Boyle, Richard. (1972) *Flower of the Dragon: the Breakdown of the US Army in Vietnam.* San Francisco: Ramparts P. p. 189

7. Bishop, Chris. ed. (1990) *Vietnam War Diary: The Month-by-Month Experience of the US Forces.* New York: Military P. p. 189

8. Perry p. 240

9. Boyle p. 75

10. ibid. p.187

11. ibid. p. 247

12. Spector, Ronald H. (1993) *After Tet: the Bloodiest Year in Vietnam.* New York: Vintage. p. 277

13. Garmise, Gayle. (1991) "Twenty Years Ago Today: Antiwar Protests Heat up in D.C." *The VVA Veteran* 11.5 p. 30

14. Nicholas H. Acheson. (1991) conversation with author, Arlington, VA

15. Maclear, Michael. (1981) *The Ten Thousand Day War, Vietnam: 1945-1975.* New York: St. Martins P. p. 281

16. Boyle p. 69

17. Garmise 11:5 p. 30

18. Garmise, Gayle.(1991) "Twenty Years Ago Today: U.S. in a "Tunnel without End." *The VVA Veteran* 11:7 p. 2

19. *Nam, the Vietnam Experience 1965-1975.* Orbis Publishers Ltd. Griffin House:161 Hammersmith Rd, London W685D. p. 461

20. Boyle p. 209

21. Garmise 11:5 p. 30

22. ibid 11:5 p. 27

23. Boyle p. 206

24. Bishop p. 97

25. Spector p. 266

26. Jacobs, Marianne. (1991) "Stats and More Stats" letter to the Editor, *The VVA Veteran* 11.3; 5+

27. McNamara, Robert S. (1995) *In Retrospect: the Tragedy and Lessons of Vietnam.* New York: Times Books

28. Newcomb, Richard. (1987) *A Pictorial History of the Vietnam War.* Garden City: Doubleday

A World of Hurt:
Between Innocence and Arrogance in Vietnam

Selected Bibliography

Barnett, Don, and Jody Foss. 1993. *Lest We Forget, Part II: the 24th Evacuation Hospital 1946-1972.* (np).

Bishop, Chris. ed. 1990. *Vietnam War Diary: The Month-by-Month Experience of the US Forces.* New York: Military P.

Boyle, Richard. 1972. *Flower of the Dragon; the Breakdown of the US Army in Vietnam.* San Francisco: Ramparts P.

Brink, Betty. 1992. "No Way Out." *Plain Dealer* (Cleveland, OH) 11 October: D1,D4

Garmise, Gayle. "Twenty Years Ago Today" *VVA Veteran.* 10.11-12 (1990): 26-27; 11,1 (1991): 27-33; 11.2:27; 11.4: 25-32; 11.5: 27-30; 11.7: 27-32; 11.7-8: 27-30; 11.10: 51-52; 11.11: 26-27; 11.12: 23-26.

Hackworth, David H. 1989. *About Face: The Odyssey of an American Warrior.* New York: Touchstone

Halberstam, David. 1972. *The Best and the Brightest.* New York: Random House

Jacobs, Marianne. 1991. "Stats and More Stats." letter to the Editor *VVA Veteran* 11.3: 5+

Karnow, Stanley. 1990. *Vietnam: a History.* New York: Viking

Lifton, Robert Jay. 1973. *Home from the War: Vietnam Veterans, Neither Victims nor Executioners.* New York: Basic.

Maclear, Michael. 1981. *The Ten Thousand Day War, Vietnam: 1945-1975.* New York: St. Martins P.

Marshall, Kathryn. 1987. *In the Combat Zone: an Oral History of American Women in Vietnam.* Boston: Little, Brown, and Co.

McNamara, Robert S. 1995. *In Retrospect: The Tragedy and Lessons of Vietnam.* New York: Times Books

————, James Blight, Robert Brigham, Thomas Biersteker and Col. Herbert Schandler. 1999. *Argument Without End: In Search of Answers to the Vietnam Tragedy.* New York. Public Affairs

Newcomb, Richard. 1987.*A Pictorial History of the Vietnam War.* Garden City: Doubleday.

Norman, Elizabeth. 1990. *Women at War: the Story of Fifty Military Nurses who served in Vietnam.* Philadephia: University of Pennsylvania.

————. 1999. *We Band of Angels: The Untold Story of American Nurses Trapped on Battan by the Japanese.* New York Random House

ORBIS Publications, Ltd. *Nam, the Vietnam Experience 1965-76.* Griffin House, 161 Hammersmith Rd., London W685D

Perry, Mark. 1989. *Four Stars: the Inside Story of the Forty-year Battle Between the Joint Chiefs of Staff and America's Civilian Leaders.* Boston: Houghton Mifflin.

Schwartz, Linda Spoonster. 1987 "Women and the Vietnam Experience." *Image: Journal of Nursing Scholarship.* 19:168-173

Sheehan, Neil. 1988. *A Bright Shining Lie, John Paul Vann and America in Vietnam.* New York: Vintage

————, Hedrick Smith, E.W. Kenworthy, and Fox Butterfield. 1971. *The Pentagon Papers.* New York: Bantam.

Smith, Winnie. 1992. *American Daughter Gone to War: on the Front Lines with an Army Nurse in Vietnam.* New York: William Morrow.

Spector, Shelby L. 1981. *Vietnam Order of Battle.* Washington, DC: US News Books.

Summers, Harry, 1982. *On Strategy: a Critical Analysis of the Vietnam War.* Novata: Presidio.

Tuchman, Barbara W. 1984. *The March of Folly: from Troy to Vietnam.* New York: Ballantine.

Van Devanter, Lynda. 1983. *Home Before Morning: The Story of an Army Nurse in Vietnam.* New York: Warner.

Walker, Keith. 1985. *A Piece of My Heart.* New York: Ballantine.

Wyatt, Clarence R. 1995.*Paper Soldiers: The American Press and the Vietnam War.* Chicago: University of Chicago Press.

Mailing List

If you would like to be informed when Mary Reynolds Powell has a speaking engagement in your area, please send your name, address and phone number to:

A World of Hurt Mailing List
c/o Greenleaf Enterprises, Inc.
PO Box 291
Chesterland, OH 44026

You may also register online at www.greenleafenterprises.com or call (800) 932-5420.

Ordering Additional Copies

To order additional copies of this book:

- Call toll-free (800) 932-5420

- Order from Greenleaf Enterprises' website at:
  www.greenleafenterprises.com

- Complete the form below and mail it to:

  Preferred Customer Dept.
  Greenleaf Enterprises, Inc.
  PO Box 291
  Chesterland, OH   44026

$14.95 ($12.95 + $2 S&H) x _____ = _____

Name _____

Address _____

City _____

State _____ Zip Code _____

Phone _____ Fax _____

Email _____

Pay by: ❑Check   ❑Visa   ❑MC   ❑AmEx   ❑Disc

CC# _____

Exp Date _____ Signature _____